Praise for *Elevate Your Excellence*

"Dave has taught hundreds of thousands of our associates over the past decade and is a master trainer on the power of doing ordinary things extraordinarily well. *Elevate Your Excellence* outlines his blueprint brilliantly."
—Shawn Meaike, President, Family First Life

"Dave once again leads us to the fundamental building blocks needed not only to pursue excellence but indeed to experience it in our everyday routines."
—Troy Tomlinson, CEO, Universal Music Publishing

"Dave doesn't motivate. He really doesn't inspire. He challenges you and invades your mind to get you to understand that the answers are inside of you. He never backs off or backs down. He brings his excellence to you in this book to bring you to places you didn't know you could get to."
—Tom Crean, ESPN College Basketball Analyst

"Dave Anderson helps you attack the problematic with practicality. His approach and teachings in *Elevate Your Excellence* provide you and your team with a road map for sustained success."
—Greg Gard, Head Men's Basketball Coach, Wisconsin Badgers

"Dave practices what he preaches. He's one of the most disciplined people I know, and I am fortunate to have played with some of the world's best and most disciplined basketball players. In *Elevate Your Excellence*, Dave shares dozens of personal stories and strategies from his life to help you add years to your life, and life to your years."
—Meyers Leonard, 10-year NBA Veteran

Elevate
Your
Excellence

Also by Dave Anderson

Intentional Mindset
Unstoppable
It's Not Rocket Science
How to Lead by THE BOOK
How to Run Your Business by THE BOOK
TKO Sales!
TKO Hiring!
TKO Management!
If You Don't Make Waves, You'll Drown
How to Deal with Difficult Customers
Up Your Business!
Selling Above the Crowd
No-Nonsense Leadership

Elevate Your Excellence

The Power of Doing Ordinary Things Extraordinarily Well

DAVE ANDERSON

Matt Holt Books
An Imprint of BenBella Books, Inc.
Dallas, TX

Elevate Your Excellence copyright © 2024 by Dave Anderson

All rights reserved. No part of this book may be used or reproduced in any manner whatsoever without written permission of the publisher, except in the case of brief quotations embodied in critical articles or reviews.

Matt Holt is an imprint of BenBella Books, Inc.
10440 N. Central Expressway
Suite 800
Dallas, TX 75231
benbellabooks.com
Send feedback to feedback@benbellabooks.com

BenBella and *Matt Holt* are federally registered trademarks.

Printed in the United States of America
10 9 8 7 6 5 4 3 2 1

Library of Congress Control Number: 2024001106
ISBN 9781637745618 (hardcover)
ISBN 9781637745625 (electronic)

Proofreading by Ashley Casteel and Marissa Wold Uhrina
Text design and composition by PerfecType, Nashville, TN
Cover design by Brigid Pearson
Printed by Lake Book Manufacturing

Special discounts for bulk sales are available. Please contact bulkorders@benbellabooks.com.

Personal Dedication

This book is dedicated to the memory of my friends Bert and Jane Boeckmann. Their lives were embodiments of excellence and testaments to the power of relentlessly and consistently doing the ordinary things extraordinarily well and thus building extraordinary lives and legacies.

Corporate Dedication

This book is also dedicated to the incredible team at PS LAX. Your ability to consistently execute the ordinary things extraordinarily well, and to master the logistics required in every aspect of air travel departures and arrivals, has elevated the excellence of my travel experience sojourning through chaotic Los Angeles International Airport for many years.

CONTENTS

Foreword by David H. Wilson **xi**

INTRODUCTION It's Personal **1**

CHAPTER ONE The "Little" Things Aren't Little Things **11**

CHAPTER TWO Nothing Is Neutral **27**

CHAPTER THREE Start Early Stacking Wins **41**

CHAPTER FOUR Master the Moment in Front of Your Face **51**

CHAPTER FIVE Resuscitate Daily Routines and Rituals **63**

CHAPTER SIX Take Ten for Mindset Mastery **77**

CHAPTER SEVEN How to Have Good "Crappy" Days **105**

CHAPTER EIGHT Drink Up! **117**

CHAPTER NINE Intentional Breathing Adds Life to Your Years **125**

CHAPTER TEN Masterful Sleeping Adds Years to Your Life **135**

CHAPTER ELEVEN Challenge Yourself **149**

CHAPTER TWELVE Elevate Yourself and Others: Write the Book **165**

CHAPTER THIRTEEN Elevate Excellence in Your Interests **175**

CHAPTER FOURTEEN Make EDMED a Lifestyle **187**

Acknowledgments **205**

Notes **207**

FOREWORD

Working with Dave Anderson has shown me irrefutable proof that we never stop evolving, and that we should never stop reaching for new levels.

As an entrepreneur and first-generation automotive dealer, I've been named to the Ford Top Volume Dealer Hall of Fame, appointed the chair of the National Ford Dealer Council, and formed countless connections and friendships over the years due to the growth of my businesses across Maryland, Delaware, and Virginia. Beyond Preston Automotive Group, which now spans twenty-six automotive dealerships, thirty-five associated rooftops, and sells nearly 16,000 retail units annually, my stakes in a digital marketing agency, home and business security company, and real estate holdings have all shared one common trait across the past fifteen years: we have shaped our leaders via the training and wisdom found within the pages of Dave's books.

It began when I learned about Dave's leadership training via a mutual friend, and I reached out to him to arrange a meeting with a small group of business leaders from Preston Automotive Group. From the very first interaction, it was clear that Dave and Preston Automotive were a perfect match. I was also humbled when Dave asked me to contribute to his 2017 book *Unstoppable: Transforming Your Mindset to Create Change, Accelerate Results, and Be the Best at What You Do*. To be able to play a role in the content of such an amazing book remains a highlight for me, and I was further grateful when Dave tabbed me in 2021 to add to *Intentional Mindset: Developing Mental Toughness and a Killer Instinct*. Furthermore, my work with Dave and attending his seminars have contributed to my role as past chairman for Provident State Bank, my current director title with Summit Financial, and my position as chairman for Triton Automotive Group.

Roll the clock to the present. Dave now spends six days a year with more than one hundred business leaders from Preston Automotive Group, iFrog Marketing Solutions, SafeHouse/Bay Country Security, and my other business ventures, which total over 1,100 employees. We come out of each session in each seminar with renewed enthusiasm for the work and new ways to lead, inspire, and achieve personal and professional goals. In between our biannual training seminars, we go into Dave's LearnToLead online training vault to continue developing our leaders and our teams, ensuring they never grow complacent due to both successes and failures.

I have read every one of Dave's books on leadership training, and I tell everyone I know that his work can be utilized as a definitive leadership manual to shape the present and future of your business and also your personal ambitions. *Elevate Your Excellence* is no exception, as it stretches the reader's limits to new levels and serves as an exemplary sequel to Dave's other work. They are all essential building blocks toward greater achievement in the business world, and I'm proud to be able to pen this message to you and bring you into Dave's latest book.

Are you ready to elevate YOUR excellence? Grab a highlighter and start reading! You will be forever grateful to Mr. Accountability, just like me!

David H. Wilson
Founder
DHW Holdings

INTRODUCTION: IT'S PERSONAL

Of my sixteen books, this is the most personal. It's personal in that it is more about improving your own life than edifying your business, and personal because I share more intimate analogies, experiences, successes, and failures from my life than in past works with hopes you'll find relevant lessons in each to help you elevate your excellence.

The book's title, *Elevate Your Excellence*, began as a keynote speech title I first delivered at LoanDepot Park in Miami, Florida, to thousands of insurance professionals from across the United States. The content for that speech, however, began many years before as strategies I developed and used in my own life and taught to my business and athlete clients in both seminars and the personal Zoom coaching sessions that populate my calendar each month. Personally experiencing the results of the actions I'll present, and seeing also how they changed the lives and careers of my clients, prompted me to take the bits and pieces relating to elevating your excellence I had scattered throughout podcasts, speeches, prior books, and full seminars, and compile them into fourteen chapters solely on the topic. Thus, I'm writing this book to convert the complete "elevate your excellence" strategies I've presented by parcel and piecemeal in various forums into a structured and comprehensive form that readers can use as their personal guide to next-level performance in all their most vital life arenas and to apply the steps most relevant to them in an order that suits their priorities and lifestyle.

The book's subtitle, *The Power of Doing Ordinary Things Extraordinarily Well*, comes from a phrase I open many of my seminars with to encourage audiences that getting to a higher performance level doesn't have to be elaborate, complicated, or fancy. It goes something like this: "Let me encourage you that you don't have to do anything extraordinary to reach the next performance level to which you're aspiring. But you will need to do the ordinary things extraordinarily well and consistently well. It's about becoming brilliant at the basics. The basics aren't intimidating. They're doable. I'm not saying they're easy, but I am saying that doing them with excellence every time regardless how you feel about doing them is worth it in the end."

HOW YOU DO ANYTHING IS HOW YOU DO EVERYTHING

I'll elaborate on the above heading soon enough in chapter one, but "how you do anything is how you do everything" is far more than a cliché or catchy phrase; it is a life-changing principle that works if you work it. And it may perhaps be your biggest takeaway from the book overall: that it *all* matters—how you think, breathe, hydrate, sleep, stay present, spend downtime, structure your day, make your bed, maintain your closet, keep your desk, groom your body, and hundreds of other "little" things that aren't so little. This is because how you do anything develops a personal standard and trains your conscience as a form of mental conditioning to either do your best or to compromise, cut corners, make excuses, or neglect a decision, duty, or discipline altogether. Then that same conscience that you've conditioned, for better or worse, with tens of thousands of "minor" decisions influences how much and how well you do in your highest-stake life arenas as well. If the "how you do anything is how you do everything" philosophy doesn't resonate or make sense yet, stick with me through chapter one, then put it to the test in your own daily routines. It can change your life.

YOU CAN BEGIN NOW

A signature sign-off I use in most of the hundreds of episodes for my *The Game Changer Life* podcast is, "There's power in now. There's no power in later. Later is overrated. You may not get later. So, get it done now!"

The strategies in this book lend themselves well to that "start now" mandate. What I present in each chapter is mostly immediately applicable and requires no effort beyond making the right decision and initiating an action within your control to pull it off. Where you begin is up to you, but as you begin and elevate your excellence, you're likely to find yourself wanting to weave more strategies into your daily routines from the various chapters, as they all lend themselves well to the "I can do this today" possibility.

THE BIG-PICTURE BUFFET

Following are the book's chapters with a very brief overview of what you can expect to find and learn.

Chapter One: The "Little Things" Aren't Little Things

This chapter explains in greater detail the principle of "how you do anything is how you do everything," how it works for you or against you, and offers twelve commonly overlooked areas of your own life to examine for excellence and potential improvement. It will also present four common lies we tell ourselves to excuse the fact that we did less than our best, which we must be aware of and renounce.

Chapter Two: Nothing Is Neutral

Chapter two gets you to take a hard look at how you spend your time and with whom you spend it through the filter that it matters *a lot* because no one and nothing has a neutral impact on your life—they take time that cannot be replaced. If even in a small way, the people you associate with and activities you engage in—both in your work arena and in your downtime—are either moving you towards your dreams or making it more difficult to get there.

Chapter Three: Start Early Stacking Wins

Here you'll discover how important it is to engage in excellence from the moment you awaken (you never have to recover from a great start), and to build personal momentum that conditions you for excellence throughout your day (and thus becomes part of your nature) so that excellence is perpetual rather than occasional or situational. Ideally, you already want to have stacked several small wins before you're in your own daily performance arena—and not wait until you're there to start trying to become excellent. This chapter shows you how.

Chapter Four: Master the Moment in Front of Your Face

Chapter four provides strategies for "being where your feet are," and for living more in the present moment—wherever that moment happens to be—and spending less time living in the past (which you can't change or control) or thinking about the future (which is purely anticipation). Since you only have personal power to elevate your excellence in the moment you're in, you must condition your mind to spend more time in those moments and to make the most of them: whether at work, at the gym, during your commute, in hobbies, or with your loved ones.

Chapter Five: Resuscitate Daily Routines and Rituals

This chapter helps you understand the difference between routines and rituals and helps you analyze and improve all your various work and non-work routines to better structure them for enhanced excellence and success. You'll conclude the chapter with an audit of your current routines and rituals, weaving in possible tweaks to improve them, and identifying unhealthy routines to eliminate altogether as well as productive routines to begin, if you haven't established them already.

Chapter Six: Take Ten for Mindset Mastery

Here you'll learn the importance of spending at least ten intentional minutes daily, preferably more, to build your mindset towards excellence, rather than leave it up for grabs and have it shaped by media negativity, the whims of the world's trends, or other wrong influences from surroundings, people, and pastimes. It also provides sample steps you can use to begin your own morning mindset routine if you don't have one already, as well as suggested enhancements you can make to a current routine.

Chapter Seven: How to Have Good "Crappy" Days

Chapter seven gives you strategies to stay engaged, move forward, and still impact results even when you're not at your best physically, when you're fighting against difficult conditions you can't control, or when baggage from your personal life weighs you down when it's time to perform.

Chapter Eight: Drink Up!

You'll learn here how simply becoming more aware of the importance of beginning the day with hydration excellence, and developing a hydration discipline to maintain it throughout the day, can improve your focus, health, mood, and mental and physical energy.

Chapter Nine: Intentional Breathing Adds Life to Your Years

This chapter teaches a simple two-and-one-half-minute box breathing technique you perform at select times during the day that keeps your body more oxygenated to aid in clear thinking, as well as reducing tension and keeping you calm in difficult moments: when facing an angry customer, in a traffic jam, while conducting an accountability conversation, or shooting a free throw in front of 15,000 hostile fans. It recommends six sets of this technique during the day and offers a layering strategy to help you easily weave this essential discipline into your life.

Chapter Ten: Masterful Sleeping Adds Years to Your Life

Chapter ten demonstrates the vast dangers to your mental and physical health of being underslept or sleeping poorly. It defines eleven various sleep and brain terms that are important to understand for masterful sleep, as well as fifteen effective tips to improve your sleep, your health, and your life immediately.

INTRODUCTION: IT'S PERSONAL

Chapter Eleven: Challenge Yourself

"Challenge Yourself" explains the value of discomfort, the necessity of leaving your comfort zone, and the benefits of doing so on such a consistent basis that you live your life comfortable being uncomfortable. This is a key to having breakthroughs of consistent growth in all your vital life arenas.

Chapter Twelve: Elevate Yourself and Others: Write the Book

You'll discover in chapter twelve the hidden benefits of daily journaling or writing and how they contribute to excellence—even if you don't like to write or don't think you're a good writer. It provides tips for developing this discipline and ample encouragement and ideas for readers who've always wanted to go beyond journaling to write a book.

Chapter Thirteen: Elevate Excellence in Your Interests

This chapter explores the importance of cultivating interests and hobbies outside of your normal vocation or profession that add a deeper sense of excellence to your life. It provides examples for how you can structure your downtime to pursue these interests and the impact they have on your aspirations for excellence overall.

Chapter Fourteen: Make EDMED a Lifestyle

Chapter fourteen explains the EDMED mindset (Every Day Means Every Day), its origin, and how it manifests in a relentless consistency that makes you unstoppable as you move towards your most essential goals. It also offers strategies for making yourself less dependent on external forces for consistency so you can become more internally driven and shift your mindset to consider consistency as a privilege, not as punishment. It concludes with a quick review of the chapter titles and encourages you to assemble or tweak your execution plan to consistently implement what you've learned from each chapter once you're finished with the book.

RECURRING THEMES

You're likely to notice early on in the book that certain themes are repeated, rephrased, and reinforced throughout these chapters. I believe in repetition to drive home key points, and I don't apologize for saying something important ten times or ten different ways if that's what it takes to make the impression needed for the reader to more seriously consider and quickly apply what I'm presenting.

TERMS TO KNOW TO HELP YOU GROW

In each chapter you'll find the following terms and topic categories. Familiarizing yourself with them now will help you know more about what to expect in each area so you can get maximum value from each of these strategic terms and chapter sections:

BullsEYE Bullet
BullsEYE Bullets (the EYE in BullsEYE representing "Elevate Your Excellence") are scattered throughout the book to add insight and emphasis to the points being made.

INTRODUCTION: IT'S PERSONAL

Some are quotes:

- **BullsEYE Bullet:** "Never become so much of an expert that you stop gaining expertise. View life as a continuous learning experience."[1]

—Denis Waitley

While others may represent a phrase or strategy:

- **BullsEYE Bullet:** Be the boxer, not the bag.

An *EYE* (Elevate Your Excellence) Opener

EYE Openers kick off each chapter with a personal story, recollection, or incident that sets the tone and provides insight for the chapter and its topic. They are all based on real-world experiences throughout my life and work journey or throughout the years of helping clients grow.

My *PEAK* (Personal Experience and Application Key)

Each chapter will wind down and conclude with my own practical experiences—good and bad—concerning the content and strategies presented within, and how I was able to apply what I'm presenting to you in practice rather than theoretically throughout my life. This is not intended as a blueprint for you to duplicate but as an example you can learn from and use as a basis for creating your own best practices.

Take Five Rapid Review and Action Steps

The final text in each chapter is a combination of five potential areas to examine in your own life, strategies to apply, or key points to remember.

It's a quick-hit summary and call to action. The five areas offered don't purport to cover all the potentially useful takeaways from a chapter, but they offer a starting place to refresh, review, refocus, and apply what's best for you.

SUPPLEMENTAL RESOURCES

If what you're reading makes sense to you, and you use it for your betterment and want to support it with further content or resources we provide, then return here for starting places:

1. Free articles and videos at the Insider Club of www.learntolead.com
2. Hundreds of episodes of *The Game Changer Life* podcast, currently downloaded in nearly two hundred nations
3. The book *Unstoppable: Transforming Your Mindset to Create Change, Accelerate Results, and Be the Best at What You Do*
4. The book *Intentional Mindset: Developing Mental Toughness and a Killer Instinct*

A BROAD LENS

Elevate Your Excellence speaks often of improving your performance in all life arenas: family relationships, workplace, social circles, downtime, hobbies, workouts, and more. If you read the pages in each chapter through that lens and look for applications in all these essential life sectors, you will exponentially compound the positive return on your efforts to leverage the power of always doing ordinary things extraordinarily well. If you're ready to grow and go, say aloud "I'm ready!" and turn the page.

Chapter One
THE "LITTLE" THINGS AREN'T LITTLE THINGS

As a young sales manager I can recall hearing Jim Rohn, who was the most influential teacher in my life at the time, say, "All disciplines affect each other. Mistakenly, the man says, 'This is the only area where I let down.' Not true. Every letdown affects the rest of your performance. Not to think so is naïve." Frankly, that seemed extreme upon first hearing it, most likely because it convicted my conscience. At the time, I wasn't paying attention to details in the "little" things in my life. In fact, I rationalized that I was so hard charging and big-picture focused that I couldn't afford to get bogged down with the minor things that took my eyes off a bigger prize. It took years for me to fully embrace the veracity of Rohn's remarks and weave them into my life.

As I tested out his principle, I did indeed find that taking shortcuts, doing less than my best, or getting sloppy in "little things"—an unmade bed, untidy workspace, disheveled personal appearance, dishes stacked in the sink, a catastrophic closet, not racking my shopping cart, a junk-heap garage, and the like—was symptomatic of more serious underlying issues that affected all aspects of my life: unproductive thinking, impotent personal standards, a conscience trained over time to permit less than my best, inadequate self-respect, poor sense of stewardship, and an anemic sense of personal responsibility. This is why "little things aren't little things." It explains how the ancient wisdom "be faithful in little things" trains our conscience towards higher standards and expectations of ourselves, which impacts our ability to positively do the bigger things with consistent excellence, whereas letting up in little things eventually impacts our performance in more vital tasks and high-stakes arenas.

If you are reflecting on what you've just read with any inkling of a guilty conscience, considering how your performance in one or more of the listed areas isn't up to par, please don't. None of what you will read in this book is about guilt or fault—even if it is your fault. It's about considering what I'm suggesting and applying it to your life, if it makes sense. If it doesn't make sense, keep doing what you're doing. If you see value in the concepts, then give them a shot to elevate your excellence.

Whatever your life aspirations—being a better parent, spouse, athlete, volunteer, manager, entrepreneur, workplace team member, spiritual leader, soldier, or student—I'd like to take some pressure off you, the same way I do my live audiences when I present this principle: You don't have to do anything extraordinary to accomplish your goal. *But*, you will need to do the ordinary things extraordinarily and consistently well. And that is something achievable for us all; I'm not saying it's easy, but that it's worth it.

THE "LITTLE" THINGS AREN'T LITTLE THINGS

> ◎ **BullsEYE Bullet:** "Perfection is what you are striving for, but perfection is an impossibility. However, striving for perfection is not an impossibility. Do the best you can under the conditions that exist. That is what counts."[2]
>
> —John Wooden

AN *EYE* (ELEVATE YOUR EXCELLENCE) OPENER: HOW YOU DO ANYTHING IS HOW YOU DO EVERYTHING

I settled into the head coach's office for a quick discussion before speaking to his team for the first time. The coach offered: "I hope you're going to talk to the team today about getting the little details right. I can see they're getting sloppy in areas away from the court, and that same 'give less than your best' standard is following them onto the court and affecting their game."

That was something I had on my agenda of points to discuss with the team, but it had already become clear to me why the players hadn't necessarily bought into their coach's words:

- The back seat and floor of the truck the coach picked me up in at the airport looked like it was one lit match away from a dumpster fire: wadded clothes, water bottles, food wrappers, and energy drink cans littered the nearly new vehicle provided by the university.
- A pile of sweatpants, hats, pennants, and banners lay on the floor in the corner of his office in such disarray that it looked like a nauseous neighborhood had vomited its annual rummage sale.
- The coach's bookshelves were covered in dust, and a golf-ball-sized stain marred the carpet on the path to the coach's desk.

It was probable the reason players were not buying into their coach's admonitions for how important details and excellence were in all things was that they didn't see *him* living it out in his own life. If he believed details matter, and talked about how details matter, then he should be conducting his own affairs like details matter. Coach hadn't made excellence in all things part of his nature but lectured the players to make it part of theirs. He was making a common leadership error of trying to export to others what he was not and take them on journeys he wasn't on. We are all prone to do likewise in our own workplace and family circles.

You'll know excellence has become part of your own nature when you raise your personal attention-to-detail standards in the "little things" across all your life arenas to the point where you wouldn't know how to do it another way; to where the practice of doing ordinary things extraordinarily well has become so natural to you that you no longer have to make a conscious effort to do them excellently.

◎ BullsEYE Bullet: To leverage the power of doing ordinary things extraordinarily well, an attitude of "doing your best in all things" must be a perpetual mindset, not a standard based on an occasional or situational whim.

Following are thoughts and points behind why little things are big deals, plus strategies for improving yourself and your personal attention to detail.

WHAT ARE YOU TRAINING TOWARDS?

Are you training your conscience towards consistent excellence, or training it to take shortcuts, to compromise, and to accept less than your best with everything you do? The importance of doing ordinary things extraordinarily well is even more compelling when one understands the connection between the decisions one makes and how those decisions train the conscience towards either excellence or compromised performance standards for oneself. When you do less than your best even in small matters, like how you keep your car or whether or not you make your bed, you, in effect, train your conscience to cut corners, compromise, or accept and expect less than your best. You then bring your one and only conscience, poorly trained, dumbed down, and compromised, into a more vital life arena—the workplace, your relationships, finances, etc.—where it then adversely influences your thinking, behaviors, and outcomes with shortcuts, compromise, and less than your best performance there too.

◎ **BullsEYE Bullet:** Low personal expectations presume and permit mediocrity. And when you accept low personal standards of performance from yourself in one area, you can start to live down to them in all areas.

A poorly trained conscience happens one failed decision or discipline at a time, and over time, it will condition you to lie to yourself to excuse and make excuses for doing less than your best in most or all things. And to reiterate, when letting yourself slack in small matters, your wrongly conditioned mind begins to slack in higher-stakes arenas of your life, like keeping a commitment to a spouse or meeting a work deadline. This is because the same compromised thinking that allowed you to not rack that shopping cart or stack dirty dishes in the sink influences and justifies letups elsewhere. While the activity may differ, the reasoning pattern is the same. The four common lies we tell ourselves when rationalizing not executing with excellence—without even thinking about the fact they aren't wholly true—are as follows, along with more realistic perspectives:

Common lie #1: *"I didn't have time to do it."* Reality: You did have the time; you just did something else with it.

Common lie #2: *"I did the best I could."* Reality: It's very unlikely you couldn't have done at least a single aspect of it even fractionally better.

Common lie #3: *"It wasn't that important anyhow."* Reality: Wrong. How you do anything is how you do everything, because the letup you just engaged in makes it easier to repeat or broaden the error.

Common lie #4: *"It's not my fault."* Reality: Of course it was. There was likely at least one aspect of your decisions or actions you could have controlled that would have avoided putting the blame on scapegoats.

MAKING EXCELLENCE PART OF YOUR NATURE

It's not crowded at the top of any field precisely because most people pay attention to detail and do their best only situationally or occasionally:

- when it is expected, or when they'll be held accountable for it;
- when someone is watching them;
- when they feel like it;
- when they're desperate;
- when there is an immediate payoff for them in some way such as gaining pleasure or avoiding pain.

Their inconsistency in striving for excellence in all things, all the time, and for setting and maintaining high standards in all their life arenas is often fueled by how they feel in the moment, rather than being influenced by the type of person they're trying to become for a lifetime.

THE "LITTLE" THINGS AREN'T LITTLE THINGS

> 🎯 **BullsEYE Bullet:** Elevating your excellence isn't about doing your best sometimes, but endeavoring to give your all consistently, in all you do, so that delivering your best always becomes automatic for you.

I can't stress this theme enough as it is the foundational principle of this chapter, so I'm rephrasing it again here: When, over time, you've committed to doing ordinary things extraordinarily well, you'll no longer have to think about it or flip on your "excellence switch." In fact, you will have striven for excellence so often and for so long that you won't know how to do anything with less than your best effort. This is how doing your best in all things, becoming a person of excellence, becomes part of your nature.

"EXCELLENCE" REDEFINED

By definition, *excellent* means *superior* or *eminent*. Within the context of this book's messages, excellence isn't about being superior to, or eminent over, anyone else or their performance. It's about continuing to be superior to your former self—who you were yesterday, the week prior, a year ago—and then persisting to strive to improve those abilities so that your bar for "doing it in a superior manner" rises. Doing everything you do with excellence doesn't mean doing everything you do exceptionally, because no one has the skills or talents to be exceptional in all things. Instead it's doing your best and giving all you have to the task at hand—and expecting your best from yourself. Excellence is holding yourself to a higher standard, and thus reshaping your mind and self-expectation to become more, do more, and achieve more in all your life arenas. It moves you mentally from doing something to "do it," or to "get through it," or so you can say that you did it, into doing it with excellence—not because someone begged or bribed you to do so, but because that's the kind of person you've chosen to be.

> 🎯 **BullsEYE Bullet:** When you do less than you can, you effectively become less than you are because you've chosen to accept less than you have to offer. In effect, you diminish yourself through neglect, indifference, and rationalization until you've conditioned yourself, over time, to expect less than you're capable of doing, and thus become less than you're capable of being.

OPPORTUNITIES TO ELEVATE YOUR EXCELLENCE WHERE "LITTLE" THINGS MATTER MAJORLY

To begin the mental conditioning that makes excellence a significant part of your nature, you're likely to find opportunities for elevating your excellence in the "hidden areas" of your life. These are aspects of your life that few people see; thus, they reflect the standards you have for yourself. In these mostly unseen areas, you're not trying to posture or impress anyone else, or gain their acceptance or approval. Some of these areas are less hidden than others, so let's dig in and evaluate what they reveal about the standards you've set for yourself and what you've trained your mind, over time, to expect and accept, knowing that this thinking and these standards will shape your performance in more visible and vital arenas; in fact, it currently is.

> 🎯 **BullsEYE Bullet:** "If you want to look good in front of thousands, you have to outwork thousands in front of nobody."[3]
>
> —**Damian Lillard, NBA player**

THE "LITTLE" THINGS AREN'T LITTLE THINGS

The inside of your automobile
Yes, the exterior matters, but weather, road conditions, and pooping birds can instantly change its complexion. The interior, particularly, is a reflection of the driver's personal standards of excellence. After all, few people see it, so what it reflects is what the owner has decided to accept for themself.

Your closet at home
Even fewer people see your closet than see the interior of your vehicle. If it is well organized and without trash, clothes, hangers, etc., scattered about, this reflects a standard you have and expect for yourself that demonstrates your wise stewardship of resources, attention to detail, and personal accountability. And you can be assured that standard carries over into the interactions you have and the work you do.

Your garage at home
You may have noticed that when most people give you a tour of their home they skip the garage, and for obvious reasons. Despite the fact that it is a significant part of one's property, it is often relegated to junk-storage status with filthy floors, scuffed walls, scattered tools, boxes, or holiday decorations. Garages are another telling aspect of someone's personal standards, as they are an easy area to compromise and keep less than your best simply because most people will never know it is in that condition.

Your back and side yards at home
Since neighbors and passersby see the front yard, it's common to pretty it up to make and maintain the right impression. But, much like your garage, few people see the back and side yards, many of which have the aesthetic appeal of a picked-over flea market.

The inside of your refrigerator, drawers, and cabinets throughout your residence
These areas are perhaps more telling than those previously mentioned, as even someone visiting your home and seeing your garage and backyard is unlikely to go through your drawers or cabinets—except, perhaps, your mother-in-law.

Your computer history
There is perhaps little better reflection of the standards you have for where you spend your time, what you allow to influence your mind and life, as well as what you value and prioritize in your down time or work time as what you've explored on your computer.

Whether you rack a shopping cart in parking lots
Being too lazy or indifferent to walk your shopping cart back to the rack demonstrates a lack of regard for another's property, and for other people's time or convenience—all of which reflect selfishness and lower personal standards of humility, attention to detail, esteem for people and property, consideration of others, and common courtesies.

The condition in which you leave a hotel room upon checking out
Is the trash in cans or scattered about the entire room? Did you clean up spills, dispose of coffee grounds, and put the used towels in a pile, and are the lights turned off? Or does the room resemble the aftermath of a junior high slumber party as you leave it a mess, rationalizing "That's not my job," as you then avoid eye contact with the housekeeper while you slouch down the hall?

THE "LITTLE" THINGS AREN'T LITTLE THINGS

Your personal grooming and appearance
While this should be a given for mature and functioning adults, it's common to see disheveled, sloppy, haphazardly groomed and dressed people futilely trying to also improve their excellence in more vital areas, build better relationships, earn promotions, acquire clients, and accomplish great things when their own grooming and dress is a walking, talking billboard for compromise, cutting corners, and low self-esteem—a visible antithesis to excellence. And excellence in this regard isn't having expensive or excellent things, but in taking excellent care of the things you have.

Your work area
While obvious, this is often overlooked. In fact, sloppy work areas are commonly justified in the name of "busyness." Letups in areas like an organized desk, desk drawers and files, shelves, and décor, etc., lead to letups in more "vital" areas essential to your daily focus and performance.

Consistency in following vital processes, executing key daily duties, and working within the discipline of sound workplace routines
You can't be attentive to details without also being consistent in their execution. Attention to detail isn't just doing things well; it's doing them well *every time*. This includes basics like being on time, conducting scheduled meetings, giving feedback, holding others accountable, sticking to a workout schedule, and adhering to processes or routines you claim are nonnegotiable.

Become more attentive to detail in your daily routines and rituals before you're at work
Great performance begins before it begins. It's difficult to make excellence and attention to detail part of your nature when you leave that

unmade bed, put garbage into your body and mind to start the day, drive a filthy car to work while listening to negative or unproductive media during your commute, cursing other drivers along the way, and the like. You can't do those less-than-excellent things and credibly walk into your workplace, "flip the switch," and magically become all about excellence and faithfulness in little things. You won't be there mentally. Be excellent in little things before you're at work, and excellence follows you into the workplace naturally.

> **BullsEYE Bullet:** Elevate your excellence by doing the ordinary things extraordinarily well, and do them regardless, so you feel better about yourself because you did them.

MY *PEAK* (PERSONAL EXPERIENCE AND APPLICATION KEY): MOTIVATED BY THE GUILT OF HYPOCRISY

All the way into my late thirties, as I climbed a business ladder that started as a sales associate and elevated to a director of operations, I'd lie to myself concerning why little things like those I've mentioned in this chapter weren't that big of a deal. I'd support my lies with an arsenal of clichés and quotes to rationalize my neglect of excellence in all things: "Don't sweat the small stuff," "Keep the big picture in mind," "I don't have time to let pennies hijack my focus from the dollars," and the like. I didn't realize I was conditioning my conscience to compromise on the excellence it would take to achieve the very big picture I pretended to value most. And to make things worse, I was quite successful despite my sloppiness in many of the ordinary things.

I moved up fast in my career, made big money at an early age, and developed a reputation as a business game changer. But despite my

THE "LITTLE" THINGS AREN'T LITTLE THINGS

efforts to minimize the importance of the little things and legitimize doing less than my best, I was distracted by a gnawing guilt and fear that my success wasn't built on a stone foundation but on sand, and that my compromising would catch up with me some day; that while I was successful, I knew I wasn't anywhere near where I could have been had I gotten my act together and pledged myself to excellence in all things instead of only the things I felt like being excellent in.

I particularly felt hypocritical teaching others about discipline, high standards, and personal accountability when I knew I fell short daily of the same principles I was admonishing them to live up to. My bed was unmade, the garage was a mess, and my closet was a laundry hamper on hangers. The good news is this created an inspirational dissatisfaction that stirred up the guilt of hypocrisy and motivated me to walk my talk.

My course correction was gradual. It took place over time, not overnight, but once I experienced the power of becoming just a little more structured, excellent, and accountable in a specific area, I began to upgrade my personal standards and expectations in more areas that snowballed and propelled me into an entirely new level of self-esteem and performance—not just on the job but in all life's arenas. I got addicted to excellence and its benefits and completely bought in to the compounding effect of better decisions, made daily, in all the vital arenas of my life. While making the "bothersome" changes first felt like I was paying a price, the ensuing increases in self-esteem, self-confidence, reputation, and results soon converted "paying" a price into "enjoying" the price. Being about excellence in all things became a daily challenge and a journey I found exciting, energizing, and rewarding.

You may be somewhere similar in your own growth journey. If so, here are some takeaways from my own experience to help support or accelerate your own trajectory:

- You don't have to change everything at once; but, by changing something for the better now, you'll want to change more over time and eventually create a compounding effect of personal growth.
- To expand further on the prior point, consider this: Transformation in standards is more of a slow-cooker process than a microwave. It happens best and lasts longest when it's a progression and accumulation of better decisions and disciplines consistently implemented over time, rather than a crash course of new tasks you take on overnight that overwhelms you and causes you to revert to your more comfortable state of rationalized mediocrity.
- You don't have to do any of the things I've suggested in this chapter and you can still be immensely successful. And at the same time, you'll fall far short of your fullest potential—the person you were designed to be, could have been, and should have been if you hadn't prioritized the status quo's comfort over the disruptive, uncomfortable journey of life-changing growth and doing your best in all things.

◎ **BullsEYE Bullet:** When you walk your talk, you don't have to talk as loudly because your actions shout excellence for you.

THE "LITTLE" THINGS AREN'T LITTLE THINGS

TAKE (5) RAPID REVIEW AND ACTION STEPS

1. "How you do anything is how you do everything" is a principle, not a cliché, because how you do what you do trains your mind to either compromise and do less than your best or to do your best every time.

2. The most telling aspects of your life that reveal the standards you have for yourself, expect from yourself, and accept from yourself, are the hidden areas that most people don't see. You do those things for YOU, and that strips away the pretense and posturing to reveal what your thinking and standards are really about.

3. Even a slight improvement or letup in a single life area, either positively or negatively, impacts other areas because of what you're conditioning your mind to strive for, accept, or rationalize as "good enough." Because of this, little things are NOT little things.

4. Making excellence "part of your nature" means you strive for excellence every time, in all life areas, to the point that you don't know how to do otherwise; it comes naturally for you.

5. Excellence isn't about being better than someone else but continually striving to be superior to your former self—consistently tweaking and reaching new personal standards that shape the person you endeavor to become.

Chapter Two
NOTHING IS NEUTRAL

As a young man in my twenties, I lacked a sense of urgency to get my act together and maximize my time because, like many young people, I fell into the trap of believing that there would always be plenty of time ... that I'd have decades ahead of me to figure out life and make my mark. I took a casual approach to time that led to casualties in my results. Embarrassingly, it wasn't until I hit my late thirties that I fully embraced a high enough regard for maximizing my time. I began to see how time spent is never replaced; it is either valued or regretted. Time is a commodity more valuable than money because you can replace lost, squandered, stolen, or spent money, but you can't get more time—even with more money. But while you can't get more time, you can redeem the time you waste or underutilize by trading it in for something more valuable. This is why to elevate your excellence, it is important to adopt a philosophy that nothing is neutral, that nothing you engage in and no one you spend time with has a neutral impact on your life. That, even if in a small way, those things or people are helping you get to where you want to go or making it more difficult to succeed in that endeavor. Why? Because everything and everyone you engage with takes irreplaceable time, and if they're taking something you cannot get more of, you should not consider their impact as neutral. Even if you engage in something you consider neither helpful nor unhelpful during the day, it is unhelpful rather than neutral because you could have done something helpful with that time instead. Thus, the "neutral" action wasn't neutral after all.

◎ **BullsEYE Bullet:** Nothing is neutral. It's either moving you forward or backward; it's not letting you "hold your own" because if it's helping you hold your own, you could have done something instead with that time that moved you forward, so, as a result, you've fallen behind.

When you begin to look at the world through the "nothing is neutral" lens, it helps create discernment that leads to better choices for what to do from when you awaken, while you're at work, and in your downtime, and to also reshape a narrower circle of friends and associates you spend quality or quantity time with: people who add value to you versus subtracting value from you.

AN *EYE* OPENER: THE HEADPHONE STRATEGY

Early in my career I'd look at my many flights from one speaking engagement to the next as "chill" time—as neutral. I saw it as a few hours when I could relax and mentally check out of work and instead watch a movie, or strike up a conversation with my seatmate, and sometimes take a nap. When I got to the hotel room after landing, I'd spend hours catching up on emails, and in class preparation for the following day's seminars or speech. As a result I'd feel behind and stressed, playing catch-up going into the evening before my class.

When I returned home from my trip, I'd work on my next book in the evening hours after supper or seclude myself at our office and do it there. This routine seemed sensible until I did an audit to determine that most months I'd spend between thirty and forty hours on airplanes in between speaking engagements—time I could be using to get ahead on work so that when I was with my team at the office, I could spend time with people work versus paperwork, and time that, when at home in the evenings, instead of separating myself from family to write, I could be with and enjoy my family. I could be in the moment and be a more excellent spouse and dad.

What I thought was a "neutral" few hours in flight that I could spend on trivial pursuits was high-potential downtime I could turn into prime time to help me reach my goals to be a better boss, writer, speaker, and family leader. "Chilling" for the thirty to forty hours per month while six miles high was not a "neutral" pursuit. In reality, my choice of how to use it caused a regression in the vital arenas I professed to value by making it more difficult to reach those goals, as I failed to utilize the time to do something that would allow me to move forward in those arenas.

After I readjusted my perspective for how to better use that time, my strategy for decades now has been to board the plane with my game face on and headphones already in place to discourage conversation with a seatmate. I have pre-scheduled the appropriate amount of productive work I can do during that allotted flight time. For instance, on a four-hour flight, I could expect to write 1,500 or so heavily proofed words for a magazine article or book chapter, as well as prep for the next day's speech or outline a podcast.

I'm all for entertainment, fun, and amusement throughout our lives, and I know how to have a good time. But to elevate my excellence in the things that matter most, I've decided to do those activities in moderation and not in excess. Instead, I've learned to prioritize building relationships, self-improvement, creating resources and personal growth in excess, as those things best align with my most meaningful life goals.

🎯 **BullsEYE Bullet:** Enjoy the trivial and amusing in moderation, and growth and impact in excess.

Building on the prior BullsEYE Bullet, consider this: If you spend two hours per night in the "entertainment" category watching Netflix with your spouse, commit to spending even more during the day or evening working on yourself—exercising, reading, listening to podcasts, taking online courses, spiritual disciplines, etc. Find ratios that work to help you maintain a productive balance between these two areas that best support reaching your goals. Pursuing this balance will also help you avoid focusing so much on work or growth that you fail to have fun, enjoy your family, your hobbies, or other interests. You can't elevate your excellence when you're "being lived" rather than truly living.

THE POWER OF PRUNING

In the opening paragraph of this chapter, I mentioned the necessity of redeeming time during the day, since you're unable to add time to your day. *Pruning* is a strategy I present in my 2015 book, *It's Not Rocket Science: 4 Simple Strategies for Mastering the Art of Execution*, that helps facilitate the execution of the daily tasks most predictive of reaching an individual's or organization's ultimate goals. This is an ideal time to discuss this technique for taking what is less than optimal in your life and making it better, one right decision and discipline at a time.

In fact, the essence of personal pruning is that you evaluate various aspects of your life, looking for areas that you consider performing as less than optimal: diet, all personal and work routines and rituals, how you use downtime, your personal associations at and away from the workplace, budget, expenses, investments, and more. Then you address each less-than-optimal area with one of the following three options.

Realign the Area

Realigning is about redirecting time or resources away from something less than optimal and into an aspect with higher potential. This is something you can't totally drop from your schedule or routine—or you can drop it but don't want to eliminate it altogether—and you realize you're spending too much time, money, etc., there and need to realign those assets into something more beneficial.

Consider these two examples:

1. You're committed to pruning your weeknight evening routines and to stop watching Netflix for three hours nightly, and instead you redeem that time with exercise, taking an online course, or reading. The challenge may be that watching television together with your spouse comprises 80 percent of the waking hours you have together during a workweek. You don't want to miss out on that traditional and limited time, nor endure the pushback from your partner about your opting to spend time you once shared together elsewhere. This would be an opportunity to maintain some time spent with your spouse while simultaneously realigning a segment of the excessive time you spend in front of the television into something more productive and predictive of

taking you to your most vital goals. Rather than give it up altogether, you start by budgeting one hour of the customary three for growth objectives and still leave two hours for entertainment and amusement. This is a solid move towards more excellently managing your time and balancing the ongoing conflict between entertainment and amusement and personal development.

2. You're managing a team and spending far too much time with an unmotivated team member who seems to want success less than you want it for him. You can't ignore the person altogether, but since you're getting a diminished return on your time, you realign some of it away from this low-return endeavor and into a coaching session with a more motivated team member with untapped talent. This time trade-off into a higher-potential team member will build excellence into your daily routine, the team member's personal growth, and the organization's maximization of human capital.

◎ **BullsEYE Bullet:** Give your best to the best and less to the rest. Avoid the tendency to weaken the strong to strengthen the weak.

Revitalize the Area

Revitalizing concerns reviving or bringing back to life something you're already doing by doing it better, adding or subtracting something to it, doing more of it, or engaging in it more often. It could be a work routine, workout routine, or daily mindset that has begun to feel stale and is having less impact than it once did.

NOTHING IS NEUTRAL

Consider these two detailed examples:

1. You're putting in a ton of hours at work and rarely take a day off, but you still fall short of production and income goals. While you can't feasibly add more hours to your current load—and probably wouldn't want to even if you could—you can make better use of the hours you're there. Thus, you reevaluate your routines and rituals during your workday, eliminate unproductive activities, schedule your priorities rather than trying to squeeze them into the day, and thereby get more from the hours you're spending there—working smarter not just harder. Working smarter not only drives excellence into your workday but can also positively elevate your relationships, as well as your physical and mental health.

2. You have a weekly date night with your spouse, which has started to get a "going through the motions" feel to it. You're both glancing at your phone constantly and talking too much about what's going on in each other's workplace and not enough time about great memories, future goals, plans, or concerns. You don't want to give up this valuable time but need to reenergize it, so you decide not to look at the phone within five minutes after getting settled at your table, nor will you discuss work topics past the appetizer being served—if at all. We all can try to do the right things and still fall short of our intended result, so rather than doing something completely different, do the same thing with more structure, intentionality, and excellence to transform it from highly rote to higher impact. That is the essence of revitalizing.

◎ **BullsEYE Bullet:** When you start doing something just to do it, or to get through it, or so you can say you did it, it's time to revitalize it.

Remove Them

Removal is ridding yourself altogether of an activity, expense, association, etc., that is having a detrimental effect on your goals, often after you've tried to realign or revitalize but to no avail. You avoid it or stop engaging in it altogether.

Consider these two detailed examples:

1. John is an old friend you constantly check in on, but whom you never get a response back from. You text, email, and forward photos of your recent activities and yet John remains a ghost. You realize you're doing all the work in what has become a one-sided relationship and decide to redirect that time, at least for a period of time, into people in your life who add value, who are responsive, and who show an interest in you by checking in on you from time to time. Thus, you choose to remove John, at least temporarily, from your check-in list. Incidentally, this doesn't mean John is wrong and you are right, or that he's bad and you are good; it's instead recognizing that continuing to invest and "water" what has at least temporarily become a "dead plant" could be a wrong, a bad use of your time in your pursuit of greater excellence and more robust relationships.

2. For years at work, you've filled out a specific report at month's end. You're good at it. You've done it for as long as you can remember, but it's not essential that you do it at all. Frankly, it's

a lower-level task you could delegate to a subordinate to stretch their abilities and make them more valuable to the company, while at the same time freeing your own time to engage in a higher-impact activity like planning, mentoring, or building your relationship with clients. Trying to get a more excellent return on your irreplaceable time isn't necessarily achieved by engaging in things you're good at, or that you've always done, or that you don't want to give up, but by asking instead, "Should I be doing this at all?" and then making adjustments as needed.

◎ **BullsEYE Bullet:** "You must constantly ask yourself these questions: Who am I around? What are they doing to me? What have they got me reading? What have they got me saying? Where do they have me going? What do they have me thinking? And most important, what do they have me becoming? Then ask yourself the big question: Is that okay? Your life does not get better by chance, it gets better by change."[4]

—Jim Rohn

PROGRESS NOT PERFECTION

It's important to balance a "nothing is neutral" philosophy with your own daily life realities and know that while there will never be "perfection" in how you invest your time or resources, you can continually make progress.

◎ **BullsEYE Bullet:** "Perfection is not attainable, but if we chase perfection we can catch excellence."[5]

—Vince Lombardi

MY *PEAK:* TRADING FORGETTABLE HOURS FOR LIFE-CHANGING MOMENTS

As this chapter opened, I discussed my poor use of what I considered "neutral" time during my dozens of hours flying to various engagements each month, and how I adjusted to maximize that time. But I also had plenty of room to optimize elsewhere during other aspects of my travel that helped me grow my results in a big way.

For additional perspective into how I recognized and corrected the error, it helps to consider that beginning in the early 2000s, my speaking and consulting schedule would easily include one hundred-plus days of various presentations in cities around the world. Add onto those engagements the associated travel days, and I was spending well over half the year on the road, and hundreds of nights in hotel rooms each year. After multiple car rides from home to airports and from airports to hotels, lines to stand in during the travel process, flights and connecting flights to catch, and the subsequent stresses and pressures involved in the journey, I'd settle in my hotel room for the evening and, after catching up on the work I should have done in flight, felt like I deserved to relax and unwind—to essentially veg and recover from the travel stresses of the day.

Consequently, I'd developed a habit to watch at least one nightly movie while eating room service, then spend some time preparing for the next day's presentation before getting a good night's sleep. Night after night, movie after movie, the hours for each year's entertainment and amusement accumulated. Those were hours I could have become more valuable with, and time I'd never get back to make that happen. While I knew the movies weren't helping me reach my goals, I rationalized that they weren't doing any harm either; it was just a "well-deserved" diversion from the busyness and stress of daily travel that would center me for the next day's speech or seminar.

After a couple years of this routine, when I was doing my annual reflection time the final week of the year, and at about the same time I added up the total hours I spent in the air flying that year, I also estimated the idle hours spent in hotel rooms, and it was staggering! My disgust compounded as it occurred to me upon reflecting that I could scarcely remember even a handful of the movies I'd seen that entire year, and I could point to even fewer quotes, lessons, or life-changing moments that arose from any of the two hours or so per night I'd mentally check out of my life and let Hollywood educate me.

At the same time, I considered the dozens of life-changing books I'd read, or productive thoughts and ideas I'd had during my better-structured air flight time, and was agitated to grasp how much better I could have become, and how much more value I could have added to family, friends, and clients, had I spent even just every other night in a hotel with structured improvement time versus amusement time. I was overweight but I didn't go to the hotel gym. I was behind in my goals but didn't learn what would give me an edge to make up the difference. I was weak in relationships but didn't take the time to reach out to, add value to, or reconnect with friends or family I'd become too busy for. I realized once again that what I thought was "neutral" was instead destructive, because if I could have been doing something productive with that time and decided not to instead, it was not neutral at all but was holding me back. Especially since it was irrecoverable.

Opting for balance, I started by reducing my movie intake by 50 percent while traveling, and structuring the other free evenings between reading, online courses, thinking time, exercise, and reaching out in relationships. In short order, the differences between what I learned and accomplished and how I felt on the growth nights became so glaringly lopsided over the amusement nights that I eliminated movies on the road altogether.

For some readers, it may not be an excess of movies but video games, bar hopping, the Food Network, Netflix bingeing, or online surfing that is compromising too much of your irreplaceable time and taking you away from taking care of your mind, body, career, and relationships. Perhaps you can find ways to redeem some of your entertainment and amusement time for activities that will make you more valuable, increase your impact, leave you feeling more fulfilled, change your own life, and help you change the lives of others. Starting small is still starting, so get going!

◎ **BullsEYE Bullet:** Measurable and consistent growth in excellence involves trade-offs, continually deciding what you must give up so that you can go up.

TAKE (5) RAPID REVIEW AND ACTION STEPS

1. Which aspects of where you spend time and with whom you spend it have you previously considered as "harmless" associations that you now realize are not having a harmless or neutral impact on your life and must be reevaluated?
2. Which of these aspects must be realigned? How will you do it?
3. Which of these aspects need to be revitalized—brought back to life or given new life? What can you do to make it happen?

4. Which of these aspects must you abstain from or eliminate altogether? When will you do it? Do you feel you have a productive balance between your entertainment time and growth time?
5. Think of life arenas where you generally "waste" time or have downtime: waiting rooms, airplane flights, nights in hotel rooms, commutes to work, etc., and think of how you can prepare in advance to use that time more excellently to move yourself towards your most vital goals.

Chapter Three
START EARLY STACKING WINS

I can recall hearing my friend and mentor, author John C. Maxwell, say in a presentation many years ago that "momentum is a leader's best friend. That when you have it, you look better than you are, and when you don't have it, you look worse than you are." John was speaking in the context of leadership training, but his principle on momentum applies to anyone at any level of performance desiring to achieve more.

So, why should you concern yourself with starting early in the day stacking wins for yourself? You earn momentum! You never have to recover from a good start. This is why to elevate your excellence daily it's best to begin from the moment you awaken by doing small tasks that build both self-esteem and self-confidence early in the day, and then carrying that momentum of confidence, excellence, and accomplishment with you into the workplace.

By stacking these wins early, and building on them throughout the day, excellence becomes more pervasive, common, and part of your nature. Unlike so many people who turn excellence on and off depending on the situation or on how they feel, excellence becomes your ongoing and expected standard in all things.

◎ **BullsEYE Bullet:** Win the first hour after waking and you can win the morning; win the morning and you're more likely to win the day.

Many people aren't excellent in a specific life "arena"—particularly their workplace—because they wait until they're *in* that place to try and do the ordinary things extraordinarily well. They're apt to: wake and get up at the last minute; leave an unmade bed; rush through their grooming; not hydrate or put anything with nutritional value in their bodies; leave their coffee cup in the sink; ignore investing even a few minutes into getting their mindset right, opting instead to poison it with social media and toxic world news, then listening to hosts debating on sports-talk radio during their commute in an unkempt car; and arrive at work a frazzled mess and somehow expect to magically shift from seat-of-the-pants slob into excellence, precision, consistency, and personal accountability. It's an unreasonable expectation that brings frustration and losses of both self-esteem and self-confidence. A poor start to each day also ensures you'll need to be deeper into the day to begin generating any momentum, and that you may not get momentum in your favor at all.

◎ **BullsEYE Bullet:** Great performance begins before it begins by stacking wins in the little things from your first waking moment, so the bigger wins come as a natural extension of your earlier momentum.

AN *EYE* OPENER: THE "MAKE YOUR BED" INTERVIEW

When interviewing a college athlete I have under consideration for inclusion in a season-long mindset mentoring process, the conversation normally proceeds similar to this simulation with "Joe":

Me: Do you do any kind of intentional breathing, or box breathing, other than when you're practicing or playing?

Joe: No.

Me: If you work with me, I'm going to teach you a box breathing routine that oxygenates your brain, puts you in the moment, and reduces tension—a routine that you'll do six times daily and the first time will be before your feet hit the floor [more on this in chapter nine]. Would you be willing to do this?

Joe: Yes.

Me: Do you make your bed in the morning?

Joe: No.

Me: If I were coming to visit you today, would you make your bed?

Joe: Yes.

Me: Why would you have higher standards for someone else than you have for yourself? If we work together, you're going to make your bed daily and send me accountability photos for two weeks. I want you to start the day with wins and doing things that most people aren't doing. You'll feel better about yourself and be reminded of your success when you return to bed in the evening and see the made bed. Do you see the value in this, and will you commit to do it without fail?

Joe: Yes, I like that.

Me: When was the last time you washed your pillowcase and sheets?

Joe: I don't remember.

Me: That's not a great answer, Joe. Do you ever have problems with acne, and if you do, does it affect how you feel about yourself?

Joe: Yes, and yes.

Me: One reason contributing to the acne may be that for what is likely a matter of months, while sleeping, you've been perspiring, salivating, oozing skin oils, and depositing thousands of dead skin cells onto your pillowcase and sheets and then spending hours nightly pressing your flesh into that cesspool. Making a bed with filthy bedding is akin to putting lipstick on a pig. I want you to wash your bedding weekly. It's another win. You'll feel better and look better too. Can you do that?

Joe: Yes, that makes sense.

Me: When do you hydrate? [More on hydration in chapter eight.]

Joe: When I get to the gym before working out.

Me: That's too late. Every morning, without fail, you wake up dehydrated because your body puts out moisture for hours and has no corresponding intake of it. Dehydration makes you sluggish, forgetful, irritable, constipated, gives you bad breath, and more. I would recommend, based on your daily activity level, that you drink sixteen ounces of water right after waking and another sixteen ounces before you leave your apartment. You'll notice an immediate difference in your energy level and alertness. Hydrating early is another win; will you do it?

Joe: Yes, that's easy.

I proceed to discuss that I'm sending him a seventeen-step, sequential, and strategic grooming process to follow every morning that creates more excellence and yet another win. (Girlfriends of athletes have thanked me for this routine in particular.) We also discuss guidelines for him to begin at least a ten-minute morning mindset routine (chapter six will expand your understanding of this vital discipline), eating something nutritional, and then protecting his freshly built momentum and mindset on the way to class or to the gym by listening to something inspirational, educational, or motivational. The new routines, rituals, and focus on living the mantra "How you do anything is how you do everything" build higher self-esteem and self-confidence that follow him into class and into his arena, improve his relationships, and more.

While I add routines over time like meditation, a pre-sleep regimen, and visualization to further maximize the mentee's time and results, what I've outlined in this chapter thus far is a sensible and meaningful starting place requiring changes that will make the person uncomfortable enough to begin growing significantly as they work through that discomfort and develop these vital daily disciplines. And while this example has related to an athlete named "Joe," it applies to anyone who strives to bring excellence into their own arena, wherever that may be.

◎ **BullsEYE Bullet:** Momentum is easier to steer than to restart. Stacking wins early creates early daily momentum that you can then steer throughout the day as excellence in all things becomes part of your nature.

SELF-CONFIDENCE AND SELF-ESTEEM

In my book *Intentional Mindset: Developing Mental Toughness and a Killer Instinct*, I discussed the differences between self-esteem and self-confidence, and the importance of both. I want to briefly review those points in this chapter (to hear an excerpt, listen to episode 228, "It's How You Finish," from my podcast *The Game Changer Life*).

In simplest terms, self-esteem is how you feel about yourself, whereas self-confidence is how you feel about your abilities. While it's common to have different degrees of each depending on what you're doing or whom you're with, the goal of elevating your excellence is to improve both the self-esteem and self-confidence that you bring with you into all situations.

In chapter five, when I discuss more about how strong and consistent routines and rituals make you feel great about yourself and also improve self-confidence in your ability to be disciplined, master new things, and follow effective processes, the impact that elevating your excellence in all things has on both self-esteem and self-confidence will become even clearer.

◎ **BullsEYE Bullet:** Self-esteem and self-confidence are fragile. No one has it all together all the time. These assets to excellence must be intentionally and consistently built by a succession of right decisions and disciplines repeated daily, even when they're hard—especially when they're hard.

MOMENTUM MAKES ADVERSITY A SPEED BUMP, NOT A SINKHOLE

You don't have to progress far in life to realize there are far more days with disappointments, setbacks, obstacles, aggravations, detours, and defeats than days when the wind is at your back twenty-four hours a day, seven days a week—when the universe is apparently dedicated to the proposition of making your life prosperous in most aspects and trouble free in all. It's also probably fair to say that everyone you know—yourself included—is going through something now either big or small that affects their performance, or has just come out of something, or is getting ready to go into something. What makes people different, over time, is how they choose to go through the adversity they encounter daily, and here is where starting early stacking wins and building both self-esteem and self-confidence each day can help: it gives you positive momentum that minimizes the inevitable negative momentum and can help you power through the daily rough spots you encounter.

If you have no positive momentum whatsoever and adversity rings your bell, you're likely to stall or regress. But with the early-earned momentum of self-confidence, self-esteem, and stacked wins, adversity is less apt to impair your progress for long, if at all. Instead, it's likely to just slow you down or momentarily distract you rather than becoming a wall you hit that stops you cold. And while you may have fortunate conditions beyond your control that either give you or accelerate your momentum, you're wise to do what's necessary to create and sustain your own momentum rather than leaving it to chance in hopes that you'll catch a break, that things will suddenly shift in your favor, or that someone will come and put you on a fast track or rescue you from difficulty.

◎ **BullsEYE Bullet:** Momentum is best, most consistent, and sustainable when it is manufactured by right daily decisions and disciplines, not when left to chance. Day in and day out, momentum must be earned.

MY *PEAK:* EARN WINS EARLY, BE UNFAZED DAILY

When I became serious about developing personal routines and rituals that stacked wins early for me each day long before I was even at my workplace, my "arena," I didn't realize an additional benefit would be that I'd be less likely to easily give way and surrender the ground I'd gained as I encountered tough spots in the workplace and throughout the course of the day. By practicing being in the moment and doing my best with the little things in the early morning hours, I conditioned my mind to follow and build on that standard throughout the day.

In fact, a few years back at LearnToLead, we created a one-word motto at our corporate offices and engraved it on a plaque we all pass by each morning as we walk into the facility. The one word on that plaque says "Unfazed." Unfazed people don't give ground. They remain unflinching when it gets tough. Staying calm and focused, they execute what they can control so they can continue to move forward regardless of the external conditions they can't control. I would contend that it is a lot tougher to remain unfazed at work when you walk into work frazzled.

The unfazed mindset was never more important to my team members and me than when the infamous California wildfires closed in on our offices and my home one November, knocking out our phone and internet service for a two-week period and causing us to live and work with the continual threat of evacuation as we conducted our daily business and served clients. Despite the crises—the fires had encroached within a mile of our offices and one hundred yards of my house—we stayed unfazed, focused on controllables, thought and spoke in terms of what we could do and what we did have, and adhered to the vital processes and structures in place that had served our company well and facilitated our growth for decades through a plethora of ups and downs.

As a result of our narrowed focus and strengthened resolve, we had our second-best month of the year that November.

If, in the midst of this crisis, we had been an undisciplined team, lacking standards of excellence and burdened by a scattered focus, prone to haphazard momentum and inconsistent execution, then crises like the wildfires, riots, earthquakes, drought, rolling blackouts, pandemic and the subsequent government shutdown of our business as nonessential, could have sidelined us or shut us down on multiple occasions.

And as you stack your own early wins each morning, you too can develop an "unfazed" mentality that makes it less likely you'll settle for less than your best as you encounter the hardship that rears its head daily. You'll be less inclined to easily give up the hard-earned ground gained and momentum you procured by doing those little things with excellence early each day that most people neglect altogether, do poorly, or think don't matter. Stacking wins early may not be enough to make you unstoppable as you progress throughout the day, but it will bring you far closer to that relentless state than if you start your mornings stumbling out of bed void of structure, leaving your mind and body up for grabs, entering work in mental disarray with no focus, no plan, and thus spending a large part of your day, day after day, winging it and reacting to the force of things happening to you, instead of being a proactive force that happens to the things around you.

◎ **BullsEYE Bullet:** Be the boxer, not the bag.

TAKE (5) RAPID REVIEW AND ACTION STEPS

1. What do you currently do consistently to start early stacking wins upon waking up each day?
2. What can you do next to start early stacking wins, even if you're not sure how to do it yet (box breathing, morning mindset routine, revised grooming routine, making your bed, etc.)?
3. What can you do to keep the wins stacking during your commute?
4. Where have you unwittingly started the day with a loss, or even stacked losses before arriving in your arena, and in effect created a negative momentum that is working against you by the time you're counted on to perform your duties with excellence?
5. Which routines for stacking wins do you currently have that have gotten stale and that you want to do better or revise completely? When will you commit to beginning?

Chapter Four
MASTER THE MOMENT IN FRONT OF YOUR FACE

For many years I've concluded the sign-off for *The Game Changer Life* podcast episodes with this admonition for urgency: "There's power in now; there's no power in later. Later is overrated. You may not get later. Get it done now!" This not-so-subtle nudge forward is to help address what is perhaps the biggest gap in life: the gap between knowing and doing. Frankly, it's easier to live in the past and think of actions you should or shouldn't have taken, or to anticipate the moves you'll make in the future when the conditions are right, in order to reach your goals. But the fact is you have no power in either of those places, and if you spend too much time there, you'll miss the *one* chance you have now to move forward, which is to master the moment in front of your face—what you can control and what you can do now in order to advance and elevate your excellence.

In my seminars, most people agree they would benefit from spending less time rehearsing, nursing, or celebrating the past, as well as less mental energy speculating about the future, in order to invest more time and energy in the present. Yet they readily admit they spend too much time everywhere other than the present. This is why staying in the moment, focusing on what you can control, and giving energy to what you have instead of to what's not real is a discipline that can and must be developed. And once you work to master this mental shift into the present, it can upgrade your performance in all life arenas.

Ironically, the folks who give too much mental space to their past or future often do so to escape a stressful or unpleasant present. Yet, by not being consistently excellent in the present, they're unconsciously planting seeds for a tougher future. We should certainly visit the past for appropriate lessons, as well as think about the future for practical planning, but practicing the discipline of being where your feet are, wherever that happens to be, is what will elevate your excellence.

◉ **BullsEYE Bullet:** Wherever you're at, be there! It's stressful and counterproductive to be in one place physically and another mentally and emotionally. You can't expect to master a moment you're not fully *in* to begin with.

AN *EYE* OPENER: POWER IN NOW FOR PETER

While discussing his key performance challenges during a coaching session, "Peter," a college athlete on the verge of turning pro, told me one of his biggest performance obstacles was "staying in the moment" and being able to let go of past successes and failures, as well as to set aside anxiety about what's next and be fully present with the task at hand. I assured him this was common, not just with the athletes I work with but was challenging for essentially anyone doing anything: whether at work, with friends or family, and even during times of solitude you set aside to recharge your mind and body. I find that people in all walks of business face the same dilemma: the salesperson is still distraught over the big deal they lost last week and is now overly consumed with where they'll end up saleswise at month's end, so much so that they're unable to even see, think in terms of, or maximize the opportunities currently in front of them that would shake them out of their funk, create positive momentum, and elevate that monthly outcome.

An athlete playing basketball who earns a trip to the free throw line is subject to the same dilemma. They badly miss their first of two shots and subsequently become so tense from beating themselves up for their error, and then worrying about "not missing" the next shot, that they get out of rhythm and miss the second shot too. They failed to mentally shift from what was or what might be to what is, to where they *do* have power and control so they could master the moment in front of their face and be successful.

Following are six suggested steps I shared with Peter that are applicable to anyone seeking to be more present, powerful, and fulfilled in the moment he or she is in.

1. Like any great performance, staying in the moment when the stakes are high begins before it begins. To make it part of one's nature, you've got to practice this discipline long before you're in your "arena"—essentially from the moment you wake up. And it takes a lot of mental conditioning to make being more present part of your nature, to where you don't even have to think about it because it comes naturally (this principle is one of the key recurring themes I suggested you notice in the introduction).
2. To start his day off "being in the moment," I taught Peter a box breathing technique that takes roughly two and a half minutes

to practice upon waking so he gets in the moment before his feet even hit the floor to begin the day (more on this in chapter nine).
3. To extend the benefits of the breathing technique, I suggested he also do a simple meditation exercise that took another two or three minutes to further condition his mind to bring his attention back to the present moment when it wandered (more on this also in chapter nine).
4. To shape his perspective, I explained that the past is only a memory trace, and that even those memories will fade and change over time, and thus, the more time he spent there, the less time he could spend in the present being his best and planting the seeds to build a better future. Gloating about a great past can make you complacent in the present, and reviling yourself over past mistakes creates tension and a lack of awareness that triggers more mistakes in the moment you're in. I also suggested that worrying about the future has the same detrimental effect, as does setting goals so far into the future that it takes the pressure off executing with excellence in the moment you're in right now.
5. I recommended he fine-tune all his daily routines to make them more strategic, sequential, and excellent to accelerate the development of the "being where his feet were" part of his nature (more on this in chapter five).
6. I shared that, like all of us, he was very unlikely to completely eliminate spending too much time mentally visiting the past or in the future. But I informed him that part of his personal growth journey would be to improve his mental discipline and awareness so that it happened less often and so that, when he did get off track, he recognized it faster and was able to gently nudge himself back into the only place he truly held any power to make a difference: his high-potential present.

> 🎯 **BullsEYE Bullet:** You gain further appreciation for the power in the present when you accept that, in a sense, the past and future are illusions; neither is a real place where you can engage and be effective. In fact, what is now your past was once made up of present moments, and what becomes your future is largely determined by whether you squander or maximize the moment in front of your face.

DON'T CONFUSE THE SCOREBOARD FOR THE GAME

I've mentioned the "Don't confuse the scoreboard for the game" mindset in several of my books, and it's a mentality that fits here very well. Think of your scoreboard as the outcomes you aspire to accomplish either daily or at some point in the future. Just as the athlete becomes less effective in the moment when he or she starts focusing too much on the score, or on how much time remains in the game, we do likewise when our obsession is more about outcomes than on executing the high-impact activity—mastering the moment in front of our face—that would move us towards that outcome.

Don't get me wrong, it is important to have outcome goals and to track your progress in any of life's endeavors: losing weight, getting in shape, saving for retirement, as well as those related to one's vocation. But if the daily execution of right activities determines whether you achieve those outcomes—and it does—then it is the "game," not the scoreboard, that requires inordinate energy, focus, effort, and obsession. In fact, when you're far ahead of where you expected to be, looking at the scoreboard can make you comfortable and shift you from playing to win to playing not to lose. And when you're behind in achieving your aspirations, fretting over the scoreboard can demoralize you and make you feel hopeless or overwhelmed. On the other hand, when you stay in the game and consistently master the moment in front of your face—knowing the right thing to do, executing it with excellence, and then moving on to the next right thing to do—the scoreboard starts to take care of itself.

Here are eight keys to help you "stay in the game" and master the moment in front of your face.

Be aware of what *the moments* are
What are your highest impact activities going into each day in your various life arenas? Know also that they may change from time to time, so to keep your focus and execution relevant and effective, you must review them frequently, lest you find yourself doing low-return things well and often—or engaging in too many things that shift your limited time away from those key actions most predictive of success. I refer to these high-impact activities in my seminars and in prior books as "Max Acts": maximum activities. The most effective way to reach your most meaningful outcomes is to become obsessed with executing the daily Max Acts that create them.

Develop exceptional skill at your highest return activities
It's not enough to simply do your Max Acts daily but to execute them with excellence, remembering that when you consistently perform the ordinary things extraordinarily well, you are helping to make excellence part of your nature.

Hold yourself accountable daily for your success in executing your Max Acts
While I'll expand on this concept in greater detail in chapter eleven, this is a good place to share some insight into this discipline. Holding yourself accountable should go beyond whether or not you executed

your priorities and should also consider how well you stayed flexible and adjusted when conditions beyond your control changed. But first and foremost, in order to hold yourself accountable, you'll need to start with clarity because clarity enables accountability; otherwise, the question becomes "Accountable for what?" This is why by beginning the day with your priorities pre-established and narrowed down, you create for yourself a benchmark for "game filming" your performance at day's end. This is simply spending a few minutes reflecting and noticing where you did well, so you can reinforce and duplicate the behaviors that enabled those wins, as well as recognizing where you fell short so you can evaluate, adjust, and be more effective tomorrow. Incidentally, this brief daily game film is an effective use of visiting the past for appropriate lessons in order to make your coming present moments more effective.

Recognize why you were successful
It's reckless to be successful without being resolutely clear as to why you were successful, because it makes it less likely you can duplicate that success consistently. As you game film and hold yourself accountable, consider what enabled your successful execution: What nonsense did you have to say no to? How were you able to regroup quickly when you did get off track? Where did your improved routines or skills pay off, and how can you continue to upgrade those assets?

Face and fix shortfalls
Game filming isn't about looking for reasons to beat yourself up but to pick yourself up so you can begin again tomorrow more intelligently. This discipline of reflecting is most effective when you take personal responsibility for why you fell short, zeroing in on the things you could have controlled but didn't, rather than succumbing to blaming other people or things for your lack of success. But notice this point emphasizes "Face

and *fix*." Improvement isn't just about making confessions: "Yep, that was my fault, I could have been more prepared." It must also include what you'll do better next time so you don't have to make the same confession concerning the same execution failure tomorrow.

Schedule tomorrow's Max Acts tonight
After game filming, look ahead to tomorrow (your next game) and consider what you'll do the same, differently, or better. It's effective to do this while shortfalls and victories are fresh in your mind. Then review the priorities you establish and schedule again during your morning mindset routine to refresh your focus (more on this in chapter six) so that when you get into your arena, you know exactly what to attack.

Be the boxer, not the bag
Above the doorway leading to my personal office is a sign that says, "Be the Boxer, Not the Bag." It's a reminder for me to be proactive, to hit the ground running and to set a productive tone for the day. And the only way I can pull that off is if I know going into my workday what I need to hit so I can set the pace, have the highest impact, create momentum, and continue the excellence and the discipline of being in the moment that I began upon waking.

Without this level of focus and resolve, I'm likely to be more like the "bag" than the "boxer": reacting to the emergencies of the moment, doing damage control, and sluggishly plodding through the day plugging holes and feeling like I'm coming from behind, making up, or trying to make up for lost ground. In that condition, I won't run the day; the day will run me.

This is also worth considering: If you're not working within the discipline of Max Act priorities at work and prioritizing the tasks that matter most, you'll probably have to spend more time at work to accomplish what you could have done in less time had you mastered the right moments in front of your face in the first place. In fact, falling short of outcome goals in any endeavor is more commonly a lack of focus than of effort. People work hard for what they want, but they don't work enough on the things that matter most.

Keep your priorities meaningful and few
Decades ago I can recall telling my supervisor, "I have ten priorities." He replied that if I had ten priorities, I didn't have a clue as to what my real job was—that I may indeed have ten important tasks to do that day, but they were not all priorities because having ten of something would destroy the entire concept of one being a priority. He wisely told me, "From the good or great things you've got to do, prioritize the best things. And be aware that it's not normally the bad things that get in the way of the best things, but those good or great things you confuse for the best things."

We commonly label just about any good or great thing we need to do as a priority, when in truth, as my boss explained, your priorities are neither good nor great things; they are the *best* things. And we should rightly remember that it's the good and great things that often edge out the best things. Of course, you must still do the good and great things, but ideally *after* you've executed the best things. And by establishing and scheduling your priorities—your Max Acts—rather than trying to squeeze them into the day or leave them to chance, you will have preestablished and planned activities to return to when you get off track and then regroup.

BullsEYE Bullet: If everything is important, then nothing is important. If you think you have "ten" priorities, you have no priorities.

MY *PEAK:* MY MARTIAL ARTS REMEDY

For too many years I was an abuser of the principles to "Be where your feet are," "Stay in the moment," and "Don't confuse the scoreboard for the game." My tendency to be in one place physically and three others mentally created unnecessary stress and an inability to fully engage with, appreciate, and enjoy what I was doing and whom I was with at the moment. To exacerbate my inconsistency at mastering the moment in front of my face, I added the extra burden of allowing past mistakes to haunt me, as I'd repeatedly replay their game tapes and overthink what I should have done differently. I also had "destination disease," where I was preoccupied with getting someplace else in the future and rarely content with where I was or what I was doing for long—anxiously chomping to move on to what was next.

In fact, I prided myself on multitasking with technology to "make things happen" on multiple fronts while I ate dinner, attended a meeting, during a day off or on vacation, or at my daughter's sporting events. The compounding stress effect of living out of the moment took a toll over time, contributing to developing ulcers, far-too-often chest pains, and a hair-trigger stress-induced temper. It also hampered my daily focus on what mattered most, leading to eventual performance plateaus.

I credit my martial arts training as one of the keys to learning to focus on what was in front of me, stay in the moment, and discipline my mind to be present. After all, thinking too much about what had just happened, or what was going on elsewhere, or what might happen later that day, normally ensured that what *did* happen to me next at the hands of my better-focused sparring partner hurt a lot and for a while. I found that the same breathing techniques, affirmations, and mental conditioning for focusing on what's most important in martial arts training were easily transferrable to staying better engaged in all of life's arenas.

It helped me work to make being present and mastering the moment in front of my face become part of my nature.

However, if I had instead developed routines and rituals and trained my mind to be more present in a life arena other than karate—at work, with friends, or at home—then that same better-trained mind would have also assisted me on the mat in karate if I had previously struggled to focus there. To reinforce once more, the principle of "how you do anything is how you do everything" is widely applicable and should encourage even small improvements in one area of your life, knowing that it will yield a positive residual effect on unrelated areas. At the same time, reminding ourselves of that principle should caution us that little letups and doing less than our best in a specific area will infect others as well.

If I had this book to read and apply decades ago, I'd have caught on to this principle much faster. The good news is that you do have it, and you can do it, and have likely already started to do so. And that's another win stacked in your day!

◎ **BullsEYE Bullet:** While you can't go back and start over again, you can begin now and create a new end.

TAKE (5) RAPID REVIEW AND ACTION STEPS

1. In which of your life arenas are you most often "out of the moment"—where you're present physically but in other places mentally and emotionally? What can you do to practice "being where your feet are" so that being in the moment becomes part of your nature?

2. How can you improve clarity for what you want to accomplish during the day so that you're able to hold yourself more accountable at day's end and evaluate and adjust where necessary?
3. What can you do to improve your daily plan? Plan the night before? Review in the morning before you're at work? Schedule your Max Acts rather than hoping to somehow fit them into your schedule? Something else?
4. In which areas of your life are you prone to become too distracted by or obsessed with the "scoreboard" and need to shift more attention to executing the key activities in that arena that are most predictive of producing the scoreboard outcome you're seeking?
5. Which of the high-impact activities is most predictive of reaching your goals, your Max Acts? Do you need to improve so that you're doing it with excellence and not just doing it to do it or get through it?

Chapter Five
RESUSCITATE DAILY ROUTINES AND RITUALS

I used to consider routines and rituals pretty much synonymous, just different terms for what I thought was essentially the same thing. It's no wonder that without understanding or appreciating the unique role of each, my routines and rituals left a lot to be desired in the pursuit to elevate my excellence. I put a lot of time into the things I wanted to get better at but didn't put enough of the right things into that time.

In this chapter I want to help you do better than I did in this regard by clearly defining the differences, the importance, and the connectedness of routines and rituals, and give you a template to evaluate your own daily routines and rituals so that you may tweak those you currently engage in to make them more excellent, eliminate unproductive routines or ritualistic steps within an otherwise solid routine, and begin routines you don't currently have that you want to start.

In simplest terms, a routine is a block of time you regularly set aside to do something, and the rituals are the steps—preferably sequential—you do within that routine. While segmenting your day into various routines is something many of us do similarly, the quality of the ritualistic steps you execute within that routine, how well and consistently you execute them, and how often you tweak them when necessary greatly determines your results.

As an example, consider that two corporate team members drive a similar distance to the same workplace five days a week, and during "John's" routine he listens to podcasts that are motivational or educational, while "Jim" tunes into political talk shows on satellite radio. Who do you think is less distracted by what they can't control, and who is more mentally focused, motivated, and prepared to perform their job with excellence upon arriving at their arena? While they have similar commute routines each day, their rituals within the routine differ greatly and thus impact the value of the routine.

And consider how common it is to see team members in nearly any workplace who work the same schedule, as in they have the same block of time where they engage at work each day, but the activities they engage in within that routine or how well they execute them—their ritualistic steps—vary greatly and determine that one is a top performer and ready for promotion, while his or her counterpart is a laggard and a candidate for termination.

The same applies to workouts at a gym, where two people go the same number of days weekly, and for the same amount of time, but one has a well-structured plan and is "all business," while the other drifts from weight station to station making small talk, watching television, checking his or her phone, and going through the motions without even breaking a sweat. They can both claim to have routines where they go to the gym X times per week for X amount of time, but their results will differ greatly based on the difference in their quality of rituals while executing their workout routine.

RESUSCITATE DAILY ROUTINES AND RITUALS

In this chapter you may discover there are some productive routines you should start or resuscitate and unproductive ones you should stop altogether. You will also benefit by reevaluating the rituals you have within each routine and consider how you can maximize the time within them. Has the routine started to feel *too* routine? Does it challenge you less than it once did? Do you do it well but lack consistency? Could you spend less time with a particular routine if you were more skilled at the rituals you engaged in, and then realign that saved time into a routine where you're inconsistent or lack meaningful engagement altogether? If all goes well in this chapter, you will identify several opportunities to elevate your excellence in your various daily routines or rituals of your life arenas. Residual benefits will include upgrading your self-esteem, self-confidence, and results simply by adding or doing those ordinary things within your routines and rituals extraordinarily well, while reducing or discarding the things you may do well but should do less of or not at all.

◎ **BullsEYE Bullet:** "The secret of your success is found in your daily routine."[6]

—John C. Maxwell

◎ **BullsEYE Bullet:** "Time management is the best kept secret of the rich."[7]

—Jim Rohn

AN *EYE* OPENER: INTENTIONAL VS. INCIDENTAL

"Billy" had been in the NBA five years when we began our work together. Billy was a people pleaser, and his challenge was keeping a positive mindset amidst his critics—of which there were plenty—and bouncing back faster from disappointments, distractions, or defeats. A common complaint concerning his performance was that he lacked confidence, and it caused inconsistency in his play. Physically, he was a "beast." His dilemma was keeping the right mindset. As a result of his inconsistency, the coach didn't trust him and would often use him sparingly, further impairing his confidence. We embarked on creating daily mindset routines that would help him grow in the right attitude and mental toughness so he could maximize his physical gifts and talents. We needed to get his mind out of the way of what his body knew how to do. We can all see this same phenomenon—underdeveloped mindset mastery because there is no intentional process in place to develop it—played out in an array of business arenas, in academics, among workers within nonprofits, and more. And like many areas where we fall short of desired results, it is entirely fixable when we put supporting routines and rituals in place.

During our multiple coaching visits, we focused on one primary strategy. And that is part of what I want to discuss in this chapter: how developing or resuscitating intentional structured routines that you execute daily can take the time you're spending already and repurpose it with more strategic intent to elevate your excellence in outcomes. While I'll go into greater detail in the next chapter concerning what you can specifically include in a mindset mastery routine, suffice it to say that by starting a routine he didn't have at all, and structuring it so he became more excellent before it was time for him to perform excellently, Billy was able to get a fresh start to his five-year career and continues to play and make millions annually in the league to this day (as of this writing).

You may also find, as Billy did, that you don't have to disrupt, discard, or begin multiple routines at once to elevate your excellence, and that by singling out just one routine or series of rituals to do extraordinarily well, you'll be encouraged to begin upgrading other life arena routines as well.

RESUSCITATE DAILY ROUTINES AND RITUALS

While you can even become overwhelmed at the prospect of all the room for improvement there is within your various life routines, keep in mind that elevating your excellence is a process, not a crash course; it's done over time, not overnight. Winning one battle at a time and then moving on to the next is going to help you win the war with your former self for greater personal excellence.

> ◎ **BullsEYE Bullet:** Sustainable excellence takes time. Remember, you're growing a person, not a weed.

EVALUATE YOUR DAILY ROUTINES AND RITUALS

In my Mindset Mastery seminar that I conduct at our Elite Center in Agoura Hills, California, I have a complete teaching section on daily routines and rituals. After explaining much of what I have thus far in this chapter, I offer our seminar guests an opportunity to evaluate their own daily routines and rituals and to ask:

- What are your normal daily routines and rituals?
- What tweaks can you make to elevate your excellence and improve each routine?
- Are there new routines you should begin that you currently lack?
- Knowing that the routines that got you "here" won't necessarily get you "there," what must change?

This exercise is a particularly effective segment of the class, as guests can begin to intentionally redesign their limited time during a day so they can better maximize their moments and elevate their results. I'll offer the same opportunity here with the following exercise, which is very similar to what we do in our Mindset Mastery seminars.

EXERCISE

ROUTINES AND RITUALS TO REVISE OR BEGIN

Evaluate and list your current routines and rituals in the space provided and outline what they are presently, and suggest potential tweaks you can make to improve them.

These routines can include but aren't limited to: wake up (before your feet hit the floor), grooming, mindset mastery, workplace commute, workday, workout, evening, pre-sleep, off-day downtime, in waiting rooms, during air travel, and more. You can also use the template to add routines you don't currently have but wish to begin. For instance, if you want to launch a workout routine but don't currently engage in one, you'd write "nothing" in the current routine and rituals spaces, and then outline ideas for what you could do and how often in the "new or revised" space. This is an ideal opportunity to evaluate and redesign the routines and rituals within your various life arenas to get more out of what you're putting into them.

1. My _____ Routine
   Describe current routine and rituals:
   _____
   _____
   _____

   New or revised routine and rituals:
   _____
   _____

RESUSCITATE DAILY ROUTINES AND RITUALS

2. **My _____ Routine**

   Describe current routine and rituals:
   _____
   _____
   _____

   New or revised routine and rituals:
   _____
   _____
   _____

3. **My _____ Routine**

   Describe current routine and rituals:
   _____
   _____
   _____

   New or revised routine and rituals:
   _____
   _____
   _____

4. **My _____ Routine**

   Describe current routine and rituals:
   _____
   _____
   _____

   New or revised routine and rituals:
   _____
   _____
   _____

ELEVATE YOUR EXCELLENCE

5. **My _____ Routine**

   Describe current routine and rituals:
   _____
   _____
   _____

   New or revised routine and rituals:
   _____
   _____
   _____

6. **My _____ Routine**

   Describe current routine and rituals:
   _____
   _____
   _____

   New or revised routine and rituals:
   _____
   _____
   _____

7. **My _____ Routine**

   Describe current routine and rituals:
   _____
   _____
   _____

   New or revised routine and rituals:
   _____
   _____
   _____

RESUSCITATE DAILY ROUTINES AND RITUALS

8. **My _____ Routine**
   Describe current routine and rituals:
   _____
   _____
   _____

   New or revised routine and rituals:
   _____
   _____
   _____

9. **My _____ Routine**
   Describe current routine and rituals:
   _____
   _____
   _____

   New or revised routine and rituals:
   _____
   _____
   _____

10. **My _____ Routine**
    Describe current routine and rituals:
    _____
    _____
    _____

    New or revised routine and rituals:
    _____
    _____
    _____

MY *PEAK:* MOVING FROM SLOP TO STRUCTURE

As a young man, my "routines and rituals" were rushed, sloppy, seat of the pants, inconsistent, and would have made a best-selling training film for how to set oneself up to fail. Other than that, they were simply outstanding! I started becoming slightly more structured in my late twenties with my first real job selling retail products. My personal responsibilities had increased, and I knew I had to tighten up my daily structure and become more purposeful and disciplined.

In my workplace I was the youngest salesman at our business, and it didn't take long for me to figure out I didn't want to end up like the "veterans" on the team, a couple of whom had worked there thirty-plus years, and while they'd grown older physically, they hadn't matured mentally. They were prone to laziness, they gushed excuses, were out of shape physically and mentally, and complained chronically about management, customers, the products, and their spouses. They gathered daily and became what I referred to as a "fellowship of the miserable."

Without my knowing what a "morning mindset routine" was, much less that I was initiating a discipline that would evolve and serve me for decades, one morning before leaving for work I decided to read a chapter of Proverbs from the Bible. I didn't have anything else in my library at the time except my Bible, and I knew the book of Proverbs was known for its wisdom. I figured a dose of right thinking taken on the way to spending time with my toxic teammates might help me stay productive. Proverbs has thirty-one chapters, so I continued reading a chapter per day (they are short) until I had finished the book in a month. And in doing so, I noticed how, as my thinking changed because of what I put into my mind, my behaviors also changed, and that those improved behaviors elevated my results on a consistent basis. In fact, I got so much out of my daily ten-minute reading that I continued to reread Proverbs every month in the same manner for years before I ever added any other steps to that morning mindset routine.

In the next chapter I'll explain how my morning mindset mastery routine has expanded over the decades, but my point here is that when you're starting a new routine of any kind, you don't have every step figured out in advance, nor does it have to be elaborate. It just needs to be effective and work well for you. As my sensei is fond of saying, "It doesn't have to be pretty, just pretty effective."

- A workout routine can start out as one ten-minute walk around your neighborhood each morning.
- You can upgrade your commute routine by deciding that for two days per week going to and from work, you'll turn off the radio and listen to something motivational or educational.
- A healthier eating routine could begin with a trade-off as simple as eating sweets just twice per week instead of twice per day.
- A personal growth routine in the evening might consist of taking one twenty-minute segment of an online course you're interested in or reading for a like amount of time—or both.
- An improved morning grooming routine could include simply using a cleanser, toner, and/or moisturizer to improve your face's skin care or a tongue scraper to remove the bacteria and food debris your toothbrush simply moves around.
- Your intentional box breathing routine as I initially mentioned in chapter three, and will explain further in an upcoming chapter, doesn't have to begin with a set six times daily, but could start with a discipline of twice per day: one set upon waking and the second set as you retire to bed for sleep in the evening.

- A more productive evening routine could be trimming your video streaming down from three hours to two hours, and replacing the one hour with exercise, an activity with your spouse, personal growth pursuits, thinking and planning time, game time with your family, and more.

◎ **BullsEYE Bullet:** "One thing is certain: if you never take the first step you will never take the second step."[8]

—Tom Ziglar

Routines and rituals will evolve over time as you find ways to improve what you're doing and determine what isn't helping you that you want to replace and which gaps you should fill for that routine to become more excellent. As I became more successful in business and could readily see the connection between the quality of my life routines and rituals and the quantity of my results, I continued to revamp them and persist to this day. I found it helpful to ask myself four basic questions regarding any routine as a precursor to improving it:

- What do I need to start doing?
- What should I stop doing?
- What should I do more of?
- What should I do less of?

In chapter seven, "How to Have Good 'Crappy' Days," I'll expand on another major benefit of effective and consistent routines: they give you something to go to and keep you on track during those tough days when you're burdened with more than the usual adversity, disappointments, distractions, or anxiety. In effect, they pull you through the tough stuff. This is why I prefer doing my ritualistic steps within a routine in the exact order every time. In addition to the sequential steps making it less likely I'll omit something, by doing the steps in the same order, I'm also more likely to stay in the moment, without confusing the scoreboard for the game, and being able to do so despite the barrage of obstacles, distractions, or difficulties I might encounter.

◎ **BullsEYE Bullet:** Look for ways to disrupt your routines. Challenge yourself; make yourself uncomfortable. Do what you're already doing that is effective with greater excellence.

TAKE (5) RAPID REVIEW AND ACTION STEPS

1. Are there unproductive routines or ritualistic steps you need to pare down or eliminate altogether? These could be instances when you're spending too much time on amusement, entertainment, or mindless activities that squander hours you'll never recover.
2. Which effective routines and rituals that you consistently perform have started to feel "too routine" and need to be tweaked? What will you do to accomplish that?
3. Is there one new routine you should prioritize to begin that you don't currently engage in? Are there more? When will you begin and what might your ritualistic steps look like to start with?
4. Is your work routine scheduled tightly enough so you don't have time to drift into trivial conversations, drama, or other low-return activities? If not, where can you tighten up your

day to focus more on priorities? It helps to remember that unmanaged time normally flows to the trivial, not to what matters most.
5. Borrowing a principle from chapter four, are there common distractions during any of your routines that take you out of the moment, and how can you work to eliminate or minimize those in advance?

Chapter Six
TAKE TEN FOR MINDSET MASTERY

For years, in my Mindset Mastery seminars, I've asked the attendees this question: "How many of you would agree that having the right mindset is more influential to success than knowledge, skills, talent, or experience?" Time after time, every hand is raised. I then follow up with this: "I agree with you. Now, based on the fact that mindset is so essential to improving your performance, how much time do you spend intentionally working to make yours better each day?" Silence and blank stares.

The group grasps as one that despite acknowledging a strong mindset's importance to elevating one's excellence, they mostly leave it to chance and do little or nothing on purpose to build or protect it.

AN *EYE* OPENER: MINDSET IS YOUR SEPARATOR

I want to be clear that when I assert that having the right mindset is more influential to success than skills, knowledge, talent, or experience,

I'm not diminishing the importance of those other attributes but rather emphasizing the fact that without appropriate and healthy thinking, one's skills, knowledge, talent, and experience can't be fully activated or leveraged.

After all, how beneficial is it to be highly skilled yet pervasively negative? Or to be greatly talented but incredibly lazy? Experienced yet complacent and entitled? Imbued with knowledge but so unfocused that it is never rightly applied?

Having a high-performance mindset is certainly the separator amongst these critical success factors. This begs the question: What do *you* intentionally do daily to build and protect your mindset? Do you daily "take ten" or more minutes for mindset mastery?

In the previous chapter I explained how I unknowingly created a daily mindset routine by simply deciding to read a chapter of Proverbs each morning before going to work. I didn't even know what a "mindset mastery routine" was at the time. All I wanted to do was think better and behave more productively so I could earn more money. But in short order, my performance began to reflect my mental investment by enabling and sustaining an attitude that demonstrated more confidence, resilience, and wisdom.

While my original intent in reading Proverbs wasn't specifically to become the top salesperson in the organization for fifteen consecutive months, I achieved the goal nonetheless as the natural result of consistently putting thoughts of positivity, possibility, and productivity into my mind. I had been "taking ten" minutes for mindset mastery without realizing that's what it was called, and the changes in my behaviors and results grew and separated my performance far above my toxic, "black belt in blame"–inclined coworkers. My sales growth served to reinforce my new mindset routine discipline and enlarged my passion to build on this routine over time. This led to me eventually weaving into my routine affirmations, daily priority goals, devotional readings, reviewing my *why*, filling out a gratitude journal, and more. Needless to say, these additions expanded my daily routine far beyond the ten minutes I read Proverbs initially, and it has become the best forty-five to sixty minutes of my day.

While I shared specifics concerning my personal affirmations and expanded upon various aspects of my morning mindset routine in my book *Unstoppable*, suffice it to say that without starting with that modest daily Proverbs reading in the first place, I'd have had nothing to add on to or to create the bigger benefits I reaped. Like any effective routine, mine evolved and improved over time to better support my growth and aspirations. Yours will likely do the same.

As a bonus, remaining consistent with this routine came easy for me because I liked how it made me feel, think, and behave, so I didn't want to skip it. And for someone like me who had a track record of inconsistency, always starting things but rarely finishing them, the ease with which this initiative became automatic was exciting. Naturally, there have been times when I've been interrupted during the routine or had emergencies arise that caused me to cut it short, but I can't recall completely skipping my "taking ten for mindset mastery" in the thirty-plus years I've had this discipline.

Over time, the success of my structured mindset routine influenced my desire to develop or improve other pre-work routines in order to compound the momentum and excellence that would, in turn, encourage me to stretch and impact my results in the workplace to ever greater levels. With each new or improved routine, my overall discipline, self-esteem, and self-confidence inched upward, as it will for anyone working daily to elevate their own mindset excellence and persisting in the consistency necessary to weave that excellence into all aspects of one's nature—to do, every day, those mundane and ordinary things extraordinarily well.

GOOD NEWS, BAD NEWS

In my book *Intentional Mindset: Develop Mental Toughness and a Killer Instinct*, I explain that your internal killer instinct gets you started towards an aspiration, while mental toughness is a measure of confidence and resilience that helps you fight through setbacks, disappointments, or defeats as you persist towards that endeavor. In addition, I demonstrate in those chapters that neither killer instinct nor mental toughness are fixed states but can be built, reinforced, and will accelerate when you work on them purposefully and consistently—ideally with supporting routines that bring out your best in those regards, especially as you work through life's adversities rather than cut corners or quit when conditions get tough. This is the good news.

At the same time, it's important to understand the less than good news. As much as this may surprise or disappoint you, your brain is inherently wired to naturally work *against* you having higher than baseline levels of killer instinct and mental toughness in order to keep you safe and help you survive. To achieve this, the brain has a negativity bias designed to mitigate the likelihood you change, engage in activities that make you uncomfortable, or otherwise take risks. Unfortunately, this wiring to live in the shallow end of the pool where it's safe, so to speak, is directly at odds with much of what I'm presenting in this book to help elevate your excellence: tasks like raising your personal standards, changing your routines, and chasing your boldest—and scariest—dreams. After all, it can be unsettling and uncomfortable to collapse your comfort zone and stretch yourself to higher performance and personal accountability levels. You may want to do it, but the brain prioritizes your comfort and survival over your happiness and works to "talk you down" from your aspirations to leave what's known and safe.

The reality of this negativity bias may help explain why it comes naturally for people who are not intentionally working against its pulling them back towards the status quo to automatically assume the worst, err on the side of caution, live in fear, and hide in the background. Many people don't realize that they're succumbing to that resistance, or why, but are merely following nature's instincts to preserve them—to add years to their life while robbing life from their years. And without a doubt, those natural survival instincts will help them get by, perhaps advance, or even succeed in the world's eyes; but, at the same time, they'll fall far short of the life of excellence and excitement they could have and should have attained, had they taken on bigger challenges, chased stretch goals, or persisted longer through difficulties.

As a suggested remedy to help you offset the brain's negativity bias and the detrimental effect it can have on reaching your goals, this chapter will provide steps to create or edify a current morning mindset mastery routine so you do the intentional daily work necessary to rewire that conditioning to "sit on the fence." You will, hopefully, learn to reprogram it instead—to get comfortable being uncomfortable, and to become your own ally rather than being at odds with yourself as you work through the change, uncertainty, and discomfort of elevating your excellence in all life arenas.

WINNING AGAINST A STACKED DECK

The importance of intentionally putting the right thoughts into your brain is made even more vital when we realize that brain activity tests show that negative memories or associations create *five times* more brain activity than positive ones, which helps explain the negativity bias I mentioned earlier.[9] Essentially, this causes you to rise every morning to work against a stacked deck; it'll take five positive experiences to balance a single negative one. Obviously, then, it's not wise to leave those five positive or productive experiences for every negative one to chance. And you're certainly not going to get the offsetting positive impressions from social media, news shows, newspapers, or during conversations with most people, many of which seem to have a degree in disempowerment and are cum laude complainers. After all, the goal isn't just to *offset* the negativity bias and break even, but to proactively overwhelm that negativity disadvantage and build a positivity bias that makes you unstoppable in your quest to see how far you can go and how much you can get out of whatever you do.

And if I may digress for a moment prior to digging into the specifics of creating or upgrading your mindset routine and ask you to consider people you know, some who may even be in your close circle of friends or members of your family, who may work hard and be well intentioned yet never seem to get ahead, and are pretty much who and where they were years or decades ago. Does anyone come to mind? A possible key to paroling them from their mediocrity isn't for them to "wait for their break" or to be rescued but is instead in having a breakthrough in their thinking; they've got their own inbred negativity bias to conquer each day. Share these keys with them and take the power for how to elevate one's thinking from "me to we." Inspire them to develop a routine that gets them out of their own way.

◎ **BullsEYE Bullet:** "If you could kick the person in the pants responsible for most of your trouble, you wouldn't sit for a month."[10]

—**Theodore Roosevelt**

A BUFFET OF OPTIONS FOR DAILY MINDSET MASTERY

I have no doubt many readers of this chapter, especially those who have read my prior books, or heard episodes of my podcast *The Game Changer Life* and attended my seminars, may already have robust and effective morning mindset routines that go far beyond taking ten minutes for mindset mastery. If this describes you, I encourage you to resist a possible "been there, done that" attitude that justifies you moving on without reading these steps. In fact, it may be the perfect time to tweak your routine or do what you're already doing with greater excellence or consistency. Stay humble and hungry and continue reading! And while the following suggestions for inclusion in your taking ten for mindset mastery each morning don't purport to comprise a complete or final word concerning the dozens of possible activities you can employ to positively affect this endeavor, they'll provide solid starting places, reminders, and ideas to customize your own morning mindset mastery disciplines.

I continually upgrade and finesse my own mindset mastery routine. In what follows, I'm offering specific, current components I utilize that go beyond what I described in *Unstoppable*. Read and evaluate which of these you currently do, or that you could do, to design or enhance your own life-changing mindset mastery routine.

Develop and Reinforce an Attitude of Gratitude

Fill out a gratitude journal to rally around and record what went right the day before. *Simple Abundance Journal of Gratitude* by Sarah Ban Breathnach is ideal for this. This is a journal I've used for well over two decades. One journal lasts one year, and there are entries to record what happened the day before that you're grateful for, as well as a monthly summary page to recount what went right during the month, which creates a unique and compelling big-picture perspective. The negative brain can wake you up with distress over what happened the day before, anxiety about the future, or disdain for what lies ahead today. Shifting your mind instead to recall, write down, rally around, and build on what was positive and productive, regardless of how small, is a momentum maker that works to offset the negativity bias and move you forward with gratitude into a new day. It's another way you can stack wins in the morning too!

Developing an attitude of gratitude, and taking the time to record it, is an engaging and meaningful discipline to share with your spouse and your children too. It can also change how you view things that don't go well, and instead of looking for a scapegoat, search for a lesson you can learn and thus be grateful for and discover in due time. In fact, I'm including an extreme example of how that can work in this section.

But despite my mentioning this aspect of a mindset routine and the impact it can have on how you approach life in both *Unstoppable* and *Intentional Mindset*, I'm often surprised in my discussions with the number of readers of both books and seminar attendees to whom I've shared this concept who've chosen not to do this. They overwhelmingly agree it makes sense, but comfortable inaction is safer for them than taking the initiative to change. Are they lazy? Indifferent? Undisciplined? Is it the cost of the journal? If a twenty-dollar gratitude journal is an obstacle, buy a two-dollar legal pad and use it, or enter your gratitude items in the Notes app of your phone daily. Find a way to make it happen. How you record and build on an attitude of gratitude daily isn't important, but *that* you do so shouldn't be an option if you're serious about offsetting a negativity bias that tends to remind you of what you still don't have, what didn't go right, and what you should be worrying about next.

In what many would perhaps consider an extreme case of looking hard to find gratitude in an event that nearly killed him, I asked my friend Sam Griesel to share his near-death story so that I could include it here. Sam, a six-foot-seven guard, played college basketball for North Dakota State University (NDSU) before transferring to his dream school, the University of Nebraska, for his final year of college eligibility. Here's what Sam shared happened while playing his final year at NDSU. If your own life experiences haven't yet convinced you that how we respond to and interpret the tough stuff that happens to us is a significant separator, perhaps his experience will.

Me: Sam, set the stage for the night you almost died in a hotel before playing a road game.

Sam: The actual incident occurred on November 11, 2021. Here's an outline of what happened leading up to the incident:

I played in an exhibition game against Minot State University and felt more tired than usual. I had played twenty-five or so minutes a game my whole career and averaged thirty-three minutes per game the year before, so I was a well-conditioned player and knew something was not right. I removed myself from the game in the first half and let my trainer know. I was examined by the doctor at the game and received positive feedback. He recommended I sit for the rest of the game but get checked out at the doctor's office the next day just to make sure. The next day, I met with a new doctor at his office and had my heart checked. Everything looked normal.

November 11th, 2021
We flew out to Cal Poly for our first official game of the year and had a walkthrough/practice in San Luis Obispo the night before the game. I felt "okay" during practice that night. I talked to my coach after practice, and we decided I would start in the game

and play my usual thirty minutes. I got back to the hotel, ate, showered, and got ready for bed. Around 10 PM I was unable to fall asleep and began to feel really hot and nauseous. I tried to make my way to the bathroom but ended up on the floor of the hotel room right outside the bathroom. I remember feeling so hot that I put my face on the tile floor to cool off. As I was lying there, I began to throw up. I vomited for a few minutes, and according to my roommate I started to yell at him to wake him up. I was lying there motionless with a pool of blood next to my head. My trainer and coach both told me later on that they were convinced I was dead due to the scene they walked into.

My trainer dialed 911 and an ambulance was there within the next few minutes. During this time, I was in and out of consciousness and was unable to sit up on my own due to the amount of blood loss. As the EMTs arrived along with firefighters, they did a quick examination and tried to get an IV in me as soon as possible, but it took about ten pokes for them to finally find the vein. With my blood pressure so low, they suspected that there was internal bleeding, so it was important to get me to the hospital. As the fluids in the IV got into my bloodstream, I became somewhat stable and could easily communicate with them. They eventually rolled me out of the hotel on a stretcher and put me in the back of an ambulance and took me to the San Luis Obispo hospital. Upon arrival at the hospital, I was rolled to the emergency side and a doctor performed a rectal exam to see what was going on. He rightly assumed the internal bleeding was coming from my stomach. At this point, I had an IV in both arms and was starting to feel better. It was 1:30 AM and I was able to call my mom to inform her of what had happened. Luckily my parents were staying in Los Angeles and could easily make the four- to five-hour trip to San Luis Obispo. Due to COVID-19 restrictions, I was basically by myself in this emergency room with random doctors and nurses. Our trainer sat with me for a bit, but after thirty minutes or so I told her to go back and get some sleep for the game tomorrow.

I didn't sleep one minute that night, and my parents eventually arrived at the hospital at 5:30 AM. It was very comforting to see them, to say the least. I stayed with them in my room with hourly checkups and blood draws until about 11 AM the next morning. The lowest my hemoglobin had gotten was 7.1. If I would've been at 7 or less, I would've needed a blood transfusion on the spot. At 11 AM, I went into endoscopic surgery to cauterize the stomach ulcer that had caused the bleeding. I came out an hour later after a successful surgery just in time to watch my team's game.

I don't really remember the game at all as I was still dealing with the anesthesia in my system, but the team pulled out a one-point victory, which made what I had just gone through the last twenty-four hours feel a little better. I stayed at the hospital the rest of the day and spent one more night. I was released the next day with my parents.

It took me nearly a month to fully recover. The recovery included a blood transfusion, an iron infusion, and several visits to the hospital to check my blood levels. I ended up making it back for the conference season and ended my playing career at North Dakota State as a First Team All-Conference Guard my senior year.

My Reflections on That Incident

Today, I'm a twenty-three-year-old professional athlete playing basketball overseas. I recently completed my fifth year of college basketball, finishing my college career playing in the Big Ten Conference at my dream school, Nebraska. When I tell people this story, the reactions are basically all the same. A lot of "Oh my gosh, I'm so sorry that happened to you" or something along those lines. It's funny because in the moment, yes, this experience was very scary, and during the recovery process, I questioned my faith and God's plan for me. But being roughly two years removed from the incident, it is clear this experience has been and will be one of the things I'm most grateful for, as I can now view it as happening for me rather than to me.

I think as an athlete, our lives are so driven by the sport we love, and it's so easy to get caught up in the work that it takes to succeed amongst our peers to the point where we literally become obsessed with the sport and forget about what really matters. I remember lying on the tile floor, not moving, not knowing what was wrong with my body, but knowing that I was in a serious situation, and all I could think about was the fact that I was going to miss the first game of my senior year. How was I going to be accepted or respected by my peers, teammates, the Summit League conference, after missing time? All I wanted was to be an all-conference player and win a conference championship and make it back to the NCAA tournament. I thought none of that would be possible because of this. How could God put me through something like this?

Then I was reminded life isn't about basketball. During my time in Fargo, I had the pleasure of meeting a young man by the name of Landon Solberg. I met Landon when he was ten years old. For the second half of Landon's life, he dealt with this thing called cancer. If you talked to Landon, you'd never know anything was "different" about him. He was a loving kid that focused on three things: loving God, his family, and his friends. Landon passed away when he was twelve years old. There's not a day that goes by that I don't think about him, and that stayed true through my incident. I was on the stretcher getting in the back of an ambulance, and I could feel Landon's presence with me. It's so hard to explain to someone that hasn't ever experienced it, but he gave me a sense of calm and belief that everything would be okay because I had an angel watching over me. From that moment on, I decided to focus on three things: loving God, my family, and my friends. Living like Landon lived. In life it's so easy to get caught up in what happens to us every day and lose the bigger picture and the perspective to it all. Since this mindset switch, I've had my two best years of my career so far and live a much more joyful life. Without the perspective of the future, it's impossible to truly know if something is good or bad that happens to us. We're all human and want to be quick to judge God or other people as the reason we may go through hardships. But focusing on what you can control through it all will lead you to a happy place.

Me: And whether you're grateful or not, or look for something to be grateful for during adversity is something you can control. Thank you for sharing, Sam.[11]

◎ **BullsEYE Bullet:** Struggles make you stronger if you look for the lesson rather than the scapegoat. Be grateful for the lessons, even if you're not grateful for what created them.

Fan Your Fire

Review your *why*. In episode eight of my *The Game Changer Life* podcast, I explained and discussed "The Power of Why." Everyone has different reasons for why they get up each morning, as well as for why anyone should even care that they get up: their purpose, goals, dreams, causes bigger than themselves, the people they're living for who depend on them, and more. To optimize your inner daily fire and focus, it's important to keep your reasons relevant and compelling, and to review them daily, ideally during your morning mindset routine. This tends to make you less dependent on external motivation by providing a heightened level of personal motivation that gets you going from the inside out. Outside motivators like recognition from others, the approval of others, and other factors beyond your control are still welcome and nice to get, they're just less necessary.

When you lose sight of your *why*, it's easy to go through life just pacing yourself, to pledge allegiance to the status quo, to quit when things get tough, to underchallenge yourself and drift from day to day going through the motions. Everyone's *why* is different; there's not a wrong or a right *why*, and once yours is clear and compelling, it will positively influence your daily decisions and disciplines and provide the internal power to flex your mental toughness muscles and keep fighting for what you want.

We offer a free downloadable *why* workbook at the Insider Club section of www.learntolead.com. This short, interactive booklet walks you through five key areas of your life that will help you clarify your *why* and serve as a basis for review during your morning mindset routine. Print copies for your spouse or teammates and do it as a joint exercise to multiply the impact of this unequalled internal motivator.

> ◎ **BullsEYE Bullet:** "You lose your way when you lose your why."[12]
> —Michael Hyatt

Affirm a Better You

Review your affirmations. A personal affirmation is a positive statement describing a trait, truth, or strategy you wish to weave into your thinking and behaviors with greater excellence and/or consistency. Choosing, creating, and then reading your personal affirmations each morning mentally moves you to think and act more like the person you're aspiring to become, so that the positive statements you've created for yourself not only shape your new reality but can evolve into being part of your nature.

For instance, if you wish to think and act less like a victim when things don't go your way, you could create an affirmation that states: "Things don't happen to me, they happen for me. I will find a way to use it and make the pain pay." With daily repetitive practice, this new way of looking at adversity can quickly shift your energy and focus away from what you can't control and into something positive and productive when you suffer a setback.

Or perhaps you're easily triggered, and you'd like to become less easy to offend. You spend too much time debating strangers on social media on topics ranging from sports to politics and religion. Your affirmation might be: "It doesn't matter, and I choose cheer." The same affirmation could be helpful in keeping your cool and maintaining calm when another driver cuts you off in traffic, someone interrupts your conversation, or a restaurant server forgets your refill.

If you're trying to become more excellent in personal accountability and want to stop blaming others or making excuses, you could employ "I own it" or "I renounce excuses." You could add to your list of affirmations over time, particularly concerning situations you don't handle well, and create an affirmation describing how you want to handle it in the future. Just as with the *why*, your affirmations are personal, don't need another's approval, and may change over time.

Be sure to use positive language because affirmations that speak in terms of what you *don't* want create stress (it's stressful to think of what you don't want, while it's energizing to affirm what you do want). For example, "I stay calm under pressure" is more positive and makes you feel far better than affirming "I don't panic and puke under pressure." In the latter case, the brain pays more attention to the outcome than the command and "panic and puke" drowns out the "don't," and you become more prone to . . . well, you know!

A basketball player launching a shot and saying to himself "Don't miss" will tense up and likely miss the shot because the thought of not missing is stressful and hearing negative commands stiffens him up and makes him tentative, but the mentality of a well-trained athlete will cause him or her to shoot successfully, thinking or saying, "points," "in," "net," "money," or something similarly positive. Or in sales, "I'm going to make this sale" is a lot more motivating than "I can't lose another sale," where the stress of "lose another sale" drowns out the "I can't."

It's common for people to tell me things like: "You've mentioned a mindset routine, affirmations, the *why*, [or a dozen other topics] in your past several books, podcasts, and seminars; I get the message! It's time to move on and talk about something new." And it's this "been there, done that" attitude concerning things they know but often don't do that holds so many people back from elevating their excellence. They know, they hear, they may even do sometimes, but they haven't mastered the task into consistency, into becoming part of their nature. If they were truly pursuing excellence, they would welcome reminders, additional insights, further discussion, and reinforcement about each and every topic essential to doing these ordinary things extraordinarily well, better than they did them the last time, and more consistently than they have in the past. After all, excellence isn't a fixed location, it's a moving target. "Learners" who accumulate information but don't often act often miss that truth, whereas "coachable" people don't just grasp the principle, they embrace and execute it.

◎ **BullsEYE Bullet:** What you say when you talk to yourself often determines what happens next with yourself.

Engage in Spiritual, Inspirational, or Motivational Disciplines

Subscribe to daily email devotionals or quotes, or read book passages that align with your personal or spiritual beliefs. Pray or meditate in a like manner if those disciplines are relevant to you. Read or listen to spiritual, inspirational, or motivational material. There are likely many podcasts you can also subscribe to in this regard.

Narrow Your Focus

Review the handful of daily priorities you scheduled the night before and must execute with excellence to move towards your personal and work goals—again, not the forty things you need to do that day, but the highest-leverage handful that you must put first. You may recall that I've referred to these priorities previously as your maximum activities, or Max Acts.

Go beyond your workplace and identify your daily Max Acts for all your life's various arenas so you're getting more from the time you invest into each area. Max Acts can often be the tough or unpleasant tasks we choose to avoid, because they unsettle our immediate desire for the gratification of doing something easier or more fun. But there's little more gratifying than getting done with excellence that handful of things that means the most. Remember that your Max Acts may change as a day progresses and new challenges or opportunities arise, but the value of a morning review during your mindset mastery routine narrows your focus to where you should start, as well as tasks that matter less to delay or say no to so you're able to execute those that matter most.

Additional Tips

Strike early

Set aside time in the morning and try to take ten for mental toughness at the same time daily. If you don't get it in early, you may not get it in at all. Besides, since this routine helps set the day's tone and stacks early wins, the earlier the better! You can also do aspects before retiring in the evening to supplement your routine, especially if your sleep chronotype predisposes you to be a night owl, and your thinking is sharper and attention more rapt in evenings than early morning. However, since what you do in the morning jump-starts your day, sets the tone, and builds momentum, you'll want to engage in morning activities as a priority. The evening option should be considered as a supplement and not a substitute.

Quiet, please

Ideally, you want to do your routine in a quiet place, free from distractions. You've got to be able to give your routine the gift of your attention, and that's inhibited when the television is blaring or kids are playing in the next room. To this end, it's also helpful to put your phone and other devices or distractions aside unless they have resources that support your routine. As basic as it sounds, if you want to maximize your morning mindset time and not just do it to do it or to get through it, you've got to *be there*; you must mentally lock in. It's not about hurrying through and ticking boxes off a to-do list but doing the things on your list with focus and thought.

Your time is the right time
There isn't a right or wrong amount of time to set aside for your routine. Make it work for you. And on days when you're rushed, you may wish to do some but not all of your tasks. Try harder to find reasons to do at least *some* of your routine rather than excuses to dismiss *all* of it. Like any habit, when you skip it once, it's easier to do it again, and then again, until you've unwound the repetition that created the habit in the first place.

Disturb your routine
You are prone to add or drop components of your routine over time as you fine-tune it to make it more effective. This is both acceptable and desirable. Don't underchallenge yourself! And when a routine starts to feel dull or rote, you're likely going through the motions and need to energize it and take it up a notch.

Turn downtime into prime time
During the spring and summer when I enjoy time in the sun by the pool, I have a regimen of memorized Bible scriptures I run through my mind and will meditate on each verse for the duration of a song playing on the sound system. When the song changes, I move on to the second, and so

forth. I typically have between forty and fifty I'll go through during my "sun and scripture" time.

I also keep my list of affirmations in the Notes app of my phone and will review some while waiting for my flights to leave, in medical waiting rooms, and in other instances of life where we're put in a position to "hurry up and wait." Be intentional and find ways to weave various aspects of your own routine to further feed your mind and spirit during prolonged times of idleness, waiting, or commuting.

Don't undo the good you did!
Keep in mind you can undo the good you do with your morning routine by engaging in counterproductive activities, media binges, web or channel surfing, associating with dramatic or moronic people, and more. A conversation I recently had along these lines with a friend progressed something like this:

My friend: I heard you deleted your Twitter account. That seems a bit crazy since you had a ton of business contacts there.

Me: Yes, I did. It caused too many unhealthy distractions throughout the day, and my best business contacts know how to find me. I deleted Twitter; it's not like I moved into a cave.

My friend: But you also primarily used it to get your news so you wouldn't need to watch news shows to stay up on world events, so how do you not become ignorant of what's happening now? Have you started watching the networks?

Me: I'd rather take a physical beating than watch the negative and dishonest network nonsense. I subscribed to www.join1440.com and it really works for me. They scour hundreds of news sources and email you a five-minute read of unbiased, "just the facts" news each morning on everything from sports and finance, to business, politics, and more. It makes me aware of what's going on without the commentary, bias, or inflammatory fluff. I can stay aware of world events without becoming obsessed by them. I've got to stay obsessed with the things I can control, and spending less time thinking and talking about what I can't control helps me do that. It's free, by the way.

My friend: But you met a lot of great people on Twitter and got some strong clients from there as well. Isn't not being there going to cost you business opportunities, marketing possibilities, and more? Don't you even feel a bit less credible as an author or speaker not having a presence there?

Me: Believe me, I thought about all that and went back and forth. We still have our corporate Twitter [@learntolead100], Facebook [@thegamechangerlife], Instagram [@learntolead100], and I maintain my personal LinkedIn. And yes, I'll miss out on some or all you mentioned, but the time I can spend instead doing what's productive will more than compensate. I look at it as a trade-off where I gave up to go up. Besides, I got tired of all the ads clogging up my stream. And I was bombarded with promoted tweets I wasn't interested in from people I never followed, and with retweets from people I did follow or like that wasted my time nonetheless. The negativity, misinformation, propaganda, and other sensational nonsense all subtracted from the good I was getting from it. I considered it carefully, as I'd had my account for fourteen years, but then decided to prune. I took what was less than optimal and removed it from my life.

By sharing this dialogue I'm offering a personal example and not suggesting anyone else needs to do the same thing. This is what worked for me when I decided that engaging in that specific forum no longer elevated my excellence nor provided an adequate return on my irreplaceable time, and I haven't looked back. Everyone needs to do what's best for them and redeem their time for something they feel is more valuable than what they're currently doing. If you're personally pleased, fulfilled, and better for doing what you're doing on social media—and believe it elevates your own excellence—and you can't think of anything else that would be an upgrade on that activity, you should certainly continue doing it until you find that "something." But don't let it become your "mindset mastery" routine. That probably won't work well for you.

Consistency is key
You wouldn't expect to build an elite body by doing five push-ups on the days you felt like it, then declaring yourself "fit for life." Nor can we build an elite mindset following the same "do it when it's convenient" or "if I feel like it" precursors to inconsistency. Many people bail out prematurely on a new discipline or activity because they're not getting a fast-enough positive consequence or payoff. They don't stick with the process long enough for the compounding effect of right decisions and disciplines done with excellence to change their lives. In many cases, they don't have strong enough reasons to stick with the discipline, so they

give themselves the option of quitting. This is where that compelling *why* positively influences your consistency. When there is a certain type of person you're trying to become, a goal or dream you crave achieving, or a difference you long to make that burns intensely, consistency will be easier, because your aspirations are so powerful that you can't afford to be inconsistent. You won't give yourself the option not to do what you need to do, because you so strongly desire what you want that you must do it.

Exercise
Intentional, consistent, well-done morning exercise is hugely beneficial. But your workout routine isn't a substitute for mindset routine, it's a supporting actor. Mind and body influence each other, and both should be made more excellent with consistently right decisions and disciplines.

◎ **BullsEYE Bullet:** If something is important enough to you, you'll find a way. If it's not, you'll find an excuse. And when your excuses muffle your dreams, you'll miss your best life.

MY *PEAK:* I DID IT FOR ME... AND FOR MY SENSEI

The martial arts, and particularly my sensei, strongly influenced both my *why* and consistency in productive disciplines for many years in unique and powerful ways that changed my life.

I was motivated to learn self-defense when I undertook volunteer mission trips to less safe parts of the world and reasoned that learning to disarm and disable assailants or kidnappers would be time well spent. I'd held an interest in the martial arts since watching Bruce Lee in the movie *Enter the Dragon* as a kid, but it was never a priority until my mid-forties when I saw a more practical purpose.

In Southern California, where I live, there are countless martial arts studios of varying styles in nearly every strip-mall shopping center throughout the Greater Los Angeles area. Many are "here today and gone in a year or two," so in my search for the right facility, I looked for the credibility of the instructor—I wanted someone who had actually fought and won in tournaments at a high level and would make his students earn it—as well as at the longevity and stability of the dojo. Good fortune smiled in a life-changing way when I discovered that my neighbor who lived two doors down was a seven-time champion in his weight class, had black belts in multiple disciplines, had been inducted into three separate karate halls of fame, was a ninth-degree black belt, and had been in business for three decades. With all those boxes checked, I enrolled in private lessons under his tutelage and went to work to learn practical self-defense. My goal initially was to learn to street fight effectively, not to progress through a rank structure and earn a black belt, but that black-belt-and-beyond goal evolved over time as I discovered I had a talent for fighting, loved contact, and caught on quickly to the techniques taught. And I credited my sensei's passion, excellence, and instructional ability with my rapid growth and love of the fighting arts. He invested so much extra time—beyond what he financially charged me for—in virtually every lesson that I never wanted to let him down. This desire became a huge part of my *why*: to affirm the belief he showed in this forty-something-year-old neighbor he spent time with on the mat (essentially every day I wasn't on the road speaking). I didn't want to invalidate his belief. I vowed to myself to pass every rank promotion test the first time for as long as I was his student. I wanted both his approval and to justify his investment, so being consistent in my nightly kata and kick-the-bag-in-the-garage practice sessions came easily. I didn't give myself the option not to do it. For well over a decade now, we've worked together regularly, and I fulfilled my goal never to fail a belt promotion, even the first-degree and second-degree black belt tests I'd seen others fail and retake multiple times. Of all the lessons I learned in business and otherwise, there was perhaps no greater teacher in my life who instilled the power of doing ordinary things extraordinarily well. As an example, in the Korean style I practice, you are required to name each kata, in Korean, with perfect pronunciation, before performing it. If you execute each move of the kata perfectly but mispronounce its name, you fail the test. The lesson: think before you speak. IT ALL MATTERS!

My motivator throughout these years wasn't primarily material in nature. Yes, I wanted the prestige and personal accomplishment of having earned a black belt rank and beyond, but my foremost motivator was of a more relational and personal nature that pushed me, as I'd never had anyone in any sector of my life put so much work into developing me. Throughout the decades, I saw clearly in my own life how having a strong *why* could fuel a level of confidence and consistency that builds the mental toughness and resilience it takes to power through the hurts, setbacks, frustrations, and disappointments throughout a long-shot journey. And those lessons were just as applicable outside the dojo in life's various arenas as they were in my *gi* on the mat. The physical and practice routines I developed raised my standard of other life routines as well, including learning to make myself more uncomfortable during my morning mindset regimen before I went to the dojo. I carried myself differently as I taught seminars, dealt with difficulties within our business, and experienced firsthand once again that "how you do anything is how you do everything," and, as you train your conscience towards excellence in a single area of your life, that influences your elevation of excellence in non-related areas as well, helping to make excellence part of your nature.

ELEVATE YOUR EXCELLENCE

Don't overlook the power of including as part of your own *why* the person or people who gave you a shot, who once did or now are investing in you. You can also include those who dismissed you, said you weren't good enough, or said that you didn't belong. Those can be powerful motivators to excel when you use their judgments as fuel to get better and prove them wrong instead of allowing them to make you bitter.

◎ **BullsEYE Bullet:** Elevating your excellence begins with how you choose to think. Change your thinking, and your behaviors change. When your behaviors change, so will your results.

TAKE (5) RAPID REVIEW AND ACTION STEPS

1. If you don't currently have a consistent morning mindset mastery routine, what would you include in yours to overwhelm the brain's negativity bias, and when will you begin?
2. If you currently have a routine, how can you make it more challenging? What could you add or spend more time on? Can you become more consistent?
3. What do you engage in during the day that helps undo the good you did with your positive mental disciplines? Too much media or social media? Unproductive screen time on televisions, phones, or computers? Unproductive or miserable people who'd like to whittle you down to their level?
4. Is your *why* clear, compelling, and current? Do you need to improve it, expand it, or perhaps download the *why*

workbook at our www.learntolead.com website and/or listen to episode eight, "The Power of Why," of my podcast *The Game Changer Life*?

5. What self-talk do you need to improve so you stop saying what you don't want and begin affirming what you do want? Sometimes we've said these things for so long we don't even realize we've conditioned our thinking so unproductively.

Chapter Seven
HOW TO HAVE GOOD "CRAPPY" DAYS

Early in my sales career I would dismiss less than good performance days with excuses like, "I didn't feel 100 percent today," or "I've got a lot going on in my personal life that's killing my focus at work," or "I barely got any sleep at all last night and never hit my stride," and more. I had a lot to learn about mastering the art of having "good crappy days."

It should go without saying that you won't elevate excellence in your various life arenas if you only put forth maximum effort on the days you feel like it, the days you are free from any physical discomfort, the days you are unencumbered by the distractions of personal issues or problems, or the days when the wind is at your back and all things you're engaged in go your way.

You may recall me mentioning in chapter five, "Resuscitate Daily Routines and Rituals," you've got to have structures established in advance that help pull you through the mundane or difficult days—"crappy days"—which, incidentally, can easily outnumber your windfall days. This helps you remain effective and productive when life throws things at you that can snuff your momentum, morale, attitude, focus, and enthusiasm, or drain your emotional and physical energy. Here's only a partial list of misery makers that help create less than good, or "crappy," days. I'm betting you recognize a few:

- Business is slow and you're falling further behind on your goals.
- You don't feel 100 percent physically.
- Relationships are strained at work or in your personal life.
- Bad news is piling up from any of your life arenas.
- Much of what you do turns out wrong or ineffective.
- You've been making one poor decision after another, and you feel snakebitten.
- You don't feel motivated or passionate about what you're doing.
- You feel stuck in a rut.
- You're putting more effort into something and getting less out of it.
- You've lost confidence.
- You don't feel great about who you are, for whatever reason, or about where you're at in your life.
- Everyone else seems to be getting the breaks or getting ahead, and that is getting into your head.
- People are ghosting you or leaving your life.
- Your financial problems worry and distract you.
- Your teenager is rebelling.
- Your health is deteriorating.
- Someone betrayed you.

HOW TO HAVE GOOD "CRAPPY" DAYS

- Your spouse drinks too much alcohol.
- Your in-laws unfairly judge you.
- Someone left you out of something you wanted to be a part of.
- Your social media wars are wearing you down.
- You're obsessed over too much you can't control.
- You feel spiritually bankrupt.
- You've been disrespected, insulted, gossiped about, or offended, and you're having a tough time getting past it.
- You've been wrongfully blamed or accused; your motives were misinterpreted.
- You've been wronged, cheated, or cheated on, and it's eating you up.
- A sick loved one or friend weighs heavy on your mind and is impairing your focus.
- You've lost a loved one.
- You feel taken for granted.
- There's something upcoming in the near future you're dreading, and it's robbing today's joy.
- Your past mistakes dominate your thoughts today.
- You didn't get the raise or promotion you were expecting.
- You were turned down for a loan.
- A friend refused the favor you requested.
- You're sick and tired of being sick and tired.

The list can and will go on. And the reality is that if you're going through any one of these conditions, or a combination of them, there are still people on your team and in your life who are counting on you to perform, to deliver on commitments, to take care of their needs, to do your share, and more, despite that it's tougher for you. And your best possible future is counting on you to get it together as well.

The chances are also very good that most everyone you're dealing with, or know, has their own "stuff" they're working through. So, the challenge for you becomes: How can you remain focused and effective during the tough moments or days, and especially those pile-on, "landslide" days when the world seems to be conspiring against your happiness, peace, productivity, and fulfillment . . . the days when you feel like a fraction of your normal self, operating at 50 percent capacity or less?

The answer: you've got to give everything you've got towards what you *do* have, to what you *can* do, to the aspects of your life you *can* control.

On those days that you feel only 50 percent effective, you need to make a mental shift and not dwell on the missing 50 percent or on what's not going right. That only serves to take you out of the moment you're in and pitch a tent on top of Mount Pity to nurse and rehearse all that's hard in your life. Instead, you get back in the present moment and be where your feet are—it's all you have for certain anyhow—and then give 100 percent of your effort to the 50 percent effectiveness or capacity you have remaining. That shifts your focus, energy, and efforts into the present moment where you can regain control, take the next one productive step you can make, and create the conditions to still salvage and bring good from a "crappy" workday, evening alone, or dinner with in-laws. The same holds for an athlete whose game isn't 100 percent to still have a good "crappy" game by finding ways to positively affect the outcome by focusing on what he or she does have or what does work, rather than being frustrated by what's not going right. After all, it's more practical to elevate your excellence, if, when you're not able to deliver excellence, you still think excellent thoughts, execute what you can control excellently, and move forward to have a positive impact.

> **⊙ BullsEYE Bullet:** Giving all you have to what you've got requires a mental shift away from the torturing aspects of life you likely cannot control and on to the decisions you can make, the action you can take, and the thoughts you can think even when you're not feeling adequate, all in, or fully engaged and effective.

AN *EYE* OPENER: YOU HAVE A JOB TO DO AND THEY'RE COUNTING ON YOU

Over the course of three decades in my public speaking career, I've never—as of this writing—missed an engagement due to travel logistical issues, injury, or illness. That is a blessing I don't take for granted, and it has helped me build a brand of excellence in dependability; although, now that I've posted this publicly, I've made it more likely the first one will occur!

There have been several events, however, where I was impaired by physical or mental conditions, sometimes severe, that made the presentations far more difficult. I needed to make it a good "crappy" presentation without the audience noticing I wasn't at 100 percent effectiveness. There was one time in particular while speaking to an audience in Columbus, Ohio (an audience I'd been with several times previously and who knew what my in-the-zone, A-game performance looked like), where this became a major challenge. It was during a pair of all-day seminars, scheduled from 9 AM to 4 PM for two consecutive days, and I suffered from severe vertigo that put me in the hospital three hours before my flight left for the event, which made it challenging to walk into the airport unassisted, much less to stand, pace, read from a workbook, and interact intelligently with an audience.

What I didn't have:

- An ability to demonstrate the same energy level they had seen in prior presentations, as the vertigo made me tentative and off-balance with my gestures
- The capacity to pace up and down the various rows of seating to interact and create a connection with the audience
- The confidence or enthusiasm that comes with feeling "100 percent normal" physically and mentally, and to convey that disposition to my audience

What I did have and what I could do:

- I asked the hotel for a stool so I could sit beside the podium occasionally, rather than stand or pace the room, and speak conversationally from that stool with the audience. The key was to do this without making it look like I needed to do it, which would have distracted the audience, but with the intention of being more conversational and intimate with a group I had developed familiarity with. It came off very naturally, and I noticed the audience even leaning in more to listen when I was seated; it got and held their attention since the approach was more personal. This sit-on-the-stool format, motivated by necessity, worked so well that I also use it in our seminars at our Elite Center training facility, where I balance and blend it with my customary pacing and standing, and reap the same benefits I did those two days in Columbus.
- The incentive and ability to prepare at greater length the evening before class, as well as in the morning prior to the seminar, so I could rely less on reading notes from the

workbook—which often appeared fuzzy anyhow. I explained the material in a more relatable manner that lent itself well to the casual "stool strategy."
- My physician provided medication that mitigated my dizziness and nausea.

The result of focusing on what I *did* have and *could* do was that the seminars were successful and engaging, without the topic of my vertigo ever coming up, and with the audience enjoying the fireside-chat style of teaching, balanced with a blend of pacing only periodically.

In life, we're all faced with performance-inhibiting conditions similar to mine, and in many instances that are far worse, that can come from nowhere, that are beyond our control, and that complicate our ability to perform at a level we know we're capable of. Our responsibility is to deal with the limitations effectively and know that elevating our excellence under tough conditions is still very possible when we focus more on the steps we can control and less on the storm we cannot. What's not a good option is mentally checking out of the situation because it's tougher, or to wait for another opportunity, or a different day to "do better." We've got to deal instead with what is, not what we wish it was, and give all we have to what we've got, even if what we have isn't impressive or ideal at the moment. Because the good news is that it is still *something*, and you've got to use that something to prevent your performance from amounting to nothing.

◎ **BullsEYE Bullet:** The Law of the Mirror: my personal decisions, more than outside conditions, determine how far I go and how fast I get there.

Following are five reinforcing and summary thoughts on having "good crappy days."

The performance "zone" everyone likes to talk about being in, and loves when they are in it, is overrated

When you're in the zone, you know it! You've got incredible focus, everything flows, things fall into place and go your way, and you can do no wrong. The problem is that you're simply not in "the zone" often enough to count on it to see you through or help you excel. You may only be in that ideal state of flow 20 percent of the time at the most, so you have two strategies to consider in that regard:

- What can you do to stay there as long as possible?
- How will you deal effectively with the other 80 percent of the time you're not in the zone?

Working to elevate your excellence in all things, having solid routines that give you something to go to when it's tough, and working (over time) so that excellence has become part of your nature will pay big dividends in these instances.

When things are tough, for whatever reason, you've got to rally around what you do have—what is working—and focus on the steps and not the storm

Stressing over what's not working is misspent focus and energy. What do you have? What can you think? Where can you focus? What can you do? How can you contribute? What can you decide and say yes or no to? Give all you do have to these aspects and those like them, and you may even shift the negative momentum you're fighting against into a positive force that facilitates a faster full-performance turnaround.

During adversity, or even when deep in a rut, you've got to maintain the mindset that while you can't always be successful, you can always get better

Elevating your excellence concerning how you think means you'll look for the gifts and lessons the difficulty is teaching you about yourself and your business, and you'll use those lessons to become stronger, wiser, and better than before. And like Sam Griesel shared, you may not see the benefits right away, but by reflecting and searching for them, you can shift your perspective from "victim" to "victor." You're not always going to be successful; no one is. But you can always get better if you keep your mindset right and don't play the victim card.

Consistent personal and performance growth aren't going to happen for you if, when things are tough, you wish it were easier, wait for a better day, or wait it out indefinitely

I'll say it again: you've got to deal with what *is*, because what *is* is your reality, despite how tough it is or how much you despise it. Elevating your excellence means learning to play well that poor hand you've been dealt, because no one is coming to rescue you or deal you a new hand! Be your own superhero and do those ordinary things you are still able to do extraordinarily well! That is what moves you forward and keeps you effective. You still may not finish where you had hoped, but you'll be far ahead of where you would have been had you surrendered to conditions you couldn't control.

By taking ten for mindset mastery each morning, you'll be better prepared in advance for "crappy days" and more prone to power through them effectively

Healthier thinking brings healthier choices, and as I've discussed previously several times and I'll repeat here for emphasis: establishing structured and effective daily routines gives you something to go to when life seems to conspire against you. They offer direction, help you stay focused and confident, and keep you moving forward, even if it is at a slower pace than you'd like or are accustomed to.

◎ **BullsEYE Bullet:** "Mental toughness is to physical as four is to one."[13]

—**Coach Bob Knight**

MY *PEAK:* YOUR BROTHER JUST DIED—NOW GET TO WORK

I was interviewed on a recent podcast and answered this question: "You've spoken in dozens of countries for three decades. Is there any *one* engagement that stands out as the toughest you've ever had to teach?" My affirmative answer to that question is the best personal example I can offer that ties together how advantageous it is to have both solid routines and rituals, and how they help you through good crappy days.

I explained how I was at home in the Los Angeles area, planning to conduct annual training for a long-term client where I would train one hundred and fifty of their leaders on various business topics, fifty at a time, over a three-day period. After awakening at my customary time of 4 AM, the phone rang at 4:15 AM with news my younger brother had died the night before. Of my four brothers, Mike was the one I was closest to. Calling the client to cancel the three days of training sessions that had been scheduled and planned one year in advance wasn't an option. My head was in disarray and my heart was broken, but I had a job to do, and one hundred and fifty businesspeople who had cleared their calendars were coming to class to learn.

In effect, I was getting ready to embark on three "crappy day" seminars with one of my most valued clients that I was determined not to let down because of a personal issue that impacted my focus and passion for being in the moment. Fortunately, I had routines and rituals to go to immediately after that devastating phone call that kept me on track and gave me some sense of normalcy and order as I struggled through the first two hours of the morning. I had a strict grooming regimen, a mindset routine, and a commute routine for the thirty-minute drive to the training venue that contributed productively to keeping me "in the game" as well.

I conducted the training those three days without ever sharing with anyone my personal issues or what I was going through, and thus distracting them from my message and diverting my own attention away from what I could control. Besides, my role was to make the sessions about the audience and not about me. Yes, at my midmorning break I went to a private office to book a flight to South Carolina for the funeral, and during my lunch hour, I coordinated with my wife to make funeral arrangements. I also wept for my brother for most of the thirty minutes home each day, but I was able to give my all to what I did have those three days in my arena and complete the training, postponing briefly the necessary grieving and healing time until their conclusion.

Much of what I've presented in the book thus far will build your own foundation and mindset, and it will prepare you in advance to help you work through your own crappy days—if you apply the principles with excellence and consistency. You can't just wish away crappy days. You're going to have your share of them. But now you can be more effective despite them.

ELEVATE YOUR EXCELLENCE

TAKE 5 — RAPID REVIEW AND ACTION STEPS

1. Define your own version of your A game, B game, and C game in your areas of performance and decide in advance what you will do when you find yourself in each situation where you must give all you have to what you've got, because what you've got isn't up to par.
2. When you're in the zone and having an A game, what can you do to stay there? Is it becoming more aware of not letting prosperity drain urgency, or rationalizing a shortcut, or doing less than you can simply because you're already doing so well? Is it something else, and if so, what, and how can you be prepared in advance to sustain your success when being successful?
3. Which routines do you need to get back to or tighten up that will help you have something to go to so you can sustain your excellence when things get tough?
4. When difficulties arise, where, what, or whom are you prone to blame concerning conditions beyond your control? Do you have "go-to" scapegoats holding you back that you need to renounce?
5. List the things you *can* control, even if the world is falling apart around you. How can you create more awareness to focus on those steps you can take and control and not on the storm you can do nothing about?

Chapter Eight
DRINK UP!

I never fully appreciated the discipline of hydration until I began practicing the martial arts and then working with athletes on improving their mental performance and physical stamina. It was common to hear people discuss the importance of staying hydrated, but I failed to recognize what actually happens to your body, and subsequently to your ability to execute the tasks you're responsible for, when you're in a dehydrated state. I was also surprised to learn how pervasive dehydration is, and that there's a 75 percent chance that as you read these words, your own body is effectively dehydrated.[14] If you don't think that's a big deal or negatively impacts elevating your excellence, then the following pages may be the most useful for you in the entire book. While this chapter is brief, it would be an error to equate its brevity with unimportance. The strategies herein can measurably change your life within minutes when you promptly apply them. But before we get to the simple remedy for the pervasive, yet fixable, affliction of hydration, consider this for the sake of perspective: Would you agree that even in a small way, some or all of the following conditions can impair your ability to perform optimally in life's various arenas and prevent you from doing ordinary things extraordinarily well?

- Lack of mental and/or physical energy
- Foggy memory
- Irritability
- Bad breath
- Constipation
- Dizziness or lightheadedness
- Cramping in your muscles
- Lack of endurance

Dehydration can inflict all of this on you, and yet the condition of being dehydrated is one of the simplest, lowest cost performance derailments you can prevent or remedy through increased awareness and intent.

To appreciate the far-reaching impact of just the first dehydration condition listed, "lack of mental and/or physical energy," consider that the definition of "energy" gives equal weight to the physical and mental aspects: *"the strength and vitality required for sustained mental and physical activity."* While physical energy relates to stamina, mental energy concerns your ability to lock in and focus on the matter at hand, to stay in the moment, and to remain there as you encounter obstacles. Considering the health and performance consequences of dehydration, making proper hydration an ongoing discipline is essential to your mental and physical health and consistent performance. And hydrating soon after waking is one of those easy wins you can stack to jump-start daily momentum.

DRINK UP!

> 🎯 **BullsEYE Bullet:** According to multiple studies, approximately 75 percent of adults in the US suffer from chronic dehydration. So, to elevate your excellence, be a 25 percenter who is hydrated and benefits accordingly! Incidentally, studies also show being just 1 percent dehydrated can cause a 5 percent decrease in cognitive brain function, increasing the motivation to elevate your excellence and pay attention to sustaining this discipline over the course of your life.[15]

AN *EYE* OPENER: LA TO SYDNEY TO WORK

Learning hydration principles early on in my business career gave me a performance edge, especially with the extensive air travel from the outset of LearnToLead's founding and continuing to this day. There's no better personal example I can offer for how it can benefit you while traveling than relating the occasion when I left from Los Angeles to Sydney, Australia, a sixteen-hour nonstop flight, for a multicity speaking tour throughout the country.

I always sleep in the early stages on international flights to give my body more time to wake up and adjust during the latter part of the flight to the upcoming destination's time zone. So, after sleeping for the first two hours after takeoff, I woke up dehydrated and began intentionally catching up.

I awoke dehydrated because while sleeping you can't drink water, of course, and while flying you are also breathing in very dry, high-altitude air brought in from the outside that accelerates your dehydration, making it particularly tough for the many folks who slept most of the sixteen-hour flight. They got up upon arrival looking like the walking dead:

commonly mumbling about jet lag, but mostly suffering from severe dehydration. Pacing myself with more water than I would normally drink during that period of time to offset the accelerated dehydration conditions, and adding in extra ounces to offset the glasses of wine with dehydrating alcohol I enjoyed with the in-flight meal, I was able to arrive at 6 AM Sydney time alert, refreshed, and able to get right to work in my hotel room preparing for the upcoming engagements.

Like so many things in life, the tools we need—like water—are readily available to us all, but lack of knowledge and/or disciplined action to apply what we know is what commonly sets us apart. That needn't be an issue for you again in this regard.

◎ **BullsEYE Bullet:** Close the gap between knowing and doing. If you don't know, you're ignorant—you lack information, training, or knowledge. If you know the right thing to do but don't do what you know, that is not ignorance; it is stupidity. Ignorance is fixable; stupidity is, well . . . you know.

EIGHT THOUGHTS, FACTS, AND STRATEGIES CONCERNING HYDRATION

1. In addition to three-quarters of us being chronically dehydrated during a day's course, it's safe to say nearly everyone awakens dehydrated because of their negative intake versus outtake of moisture during their several hours of sleep as they breathe out and perspire moisture with no corresponding hydration. So, to elevate your excellence and become more of a "morning person" who bursts into the day faster and with more energy, drink your

water in the morning before you drink your coffee, which, if it is caffeinated, will dehydrate you further!
2. When you're dehydrated, your blood thickens and your organs slow down. Thus, it takes more energy to simply pump your blood to perform normal bodily functions. This is why you commonly feel more tired or drained than you should be in proportion to the amount of activity you exert; additional energy is being used just to work your organs and perform standard bodily functions.
3. As previously mentioned, drinking alcohol, caffeine, and energy drinks accelerates dehydration. Thus, be aware and drink more water when you imbibe these enemies of hydration.
4. Develop a daily hydration discipline. I recommend to my coaching and seminar clients that they start their morning discipline by drinking eight to sixteen ounces, depending upon their size and activity level, soon after waking.
5. Air travel accelerates dehydration. This is because an estimated 70 percent of the air is brought in from the outside at high altitudes, and that air is extremely dry. It quickly dehydrates you, and the effect is exacerbated if you're drinking caffeine or alcohol before you board the plane or while in flight but not drinking water too. These conditions create the perfect storm for symptoms normally mistaken as "jet lag," whose symptoms are similar to dehydration.
6. There is not a "set" amount of water you should drink, as it can vary based on your physical activity and size. Ask your doctor during your next physical, and they may suggest somewhere between 96 and 128 ounces daily. Thus, you'll need to develop a discipline to monitor your water intake during the day.

7. Avoid drinking too much water close to bedtime. Knowing that you'll awaken dehydrated, it's intuitive to believe you're wise to load up on water before retiring for the evening. However, if it disrupts your sleep by waking you to go to the bathroom and you can't go back to sleep, it's hurting your health. The fact is: You don't need a good memory, strong focus, or physical or mental energy while sleeping. In other words, it's okay not to be fully hydrated in a state of slumber—you're resting, you're not performing—so draw back on the liquids as you approach sleep time. Just hydrate quickly after rising.

8. Don't go overboard. Be aware that drinking too much water can be detrimental to your health. It can reduce your sodium levels, which, among other things, can cause a disoriented state. It can also put undue stress on your kidneys as they must process and flush excessive fluids. I had personally gotten into the habit of drinking nearly two gallons of water per day, which, based on my activity level, was excessive. I never knew too much water could be a bad thing! But during an annual physical, my doctor was alarmed that my blood work, which usually came back normal in all categories, was way off in the kidney metric. He suspected too much liquid intake, asked how much I drank, then suggested I dial back to drinking one gallon on days I'm not traveling, speaking, or engaging in martial arts. During my follow-up checkup ninety days later, my kidney number was back in the normal range. Again, checking with a doctor to find your optimal suggested intake is wise.

◎ BullsEYE Bullet: Hydrate or deteriorate: a daily choice.

MY *PEAK:* HYDRATE FIRST, DRINK TO THIRST

Building on the advice to dial back my excessive water intake in the prior point, my doctor shared this simple philosophy: hydrate first, drink to thirst. In other words, drink more water early in the day, especially soon after waking up when you're dehydrated, and from thereon out strictly drink to thirst. He told me to avoid mindlessly sipping from a cup throughout the day if I wasn't thirsty, which is what I tended to do soon after my early-morning immersion to jump-start hydration; I'd have a thirty-two-ounce bottle on my desk and whittle it down repeatedly throughout the course of the day, even when I wasn't thirsty. His "hydrate first, drink to thirst" philosophy made sense to me, was strategic, and has worked well based on the results of my subsequent checkups and blood work, where my kidney numbers remain normal, while I have optimal energy throughout the day.

If you are highly active during the day, I want to stress that the early-morning hydration is especially a key, so much so that I suggest it as part of the morning routine for the athletes I work with; many of whom aren't accustomed to hydrating until they get into the gym. But when you examine the benefits of hydration, and the penalties of being dehydrated, the same "drink sixteen ounces within the first two hours after waking," or something of that nature, should apply to anyone in any vocation wanting to elevate their excellence and get locked into the right energy and focus upon waking and preparing to perform with excellence.

◎ **BullsEYE Bullet:** The healthiest, most effective energy drink isn't an "energy drink." It's water.

TAKE (5) RAPID REVIEW AND ACTION STEPS

1. Do you hydrate to jump-start your day and drink water before drinking caffeinated beverages like coffee, tea, or soda? If any of the dehydration symptoms listed affect you, reevaluating how much water you drink overall, and especially in relation to the caffeine or alcohol you take in, may nudge you to make an adjustment. It might be an easy fix and an ideal time to do an ordinary activity like drinking water extraordinarily well.

2. Is incorporating a more intentional water intake as part of your early-morning routine something worth considering? How far into the day do you currently wait before drinking water? Do you need water right now to combat dehydration?

3. Should you cut back on liquid intake late in the evening to improve your sleep rhythm? Does it make sense that it's not necessary to be completely hydrated throughout the duration of your sleep time?

4. Do you drink too much water based on your size and activity level, and is this something you should discuss with a doctor during your next visit?

5. Be particularly aware of the importance of hydration when visiting or living in higher altitudes, enduring dehydrating climates, and when traveling by air. Be more intentional, and you'll be more excellent and effective when you arrive and throughout your stay.

Chapter Nine

INTENTIONAL BREATHING ADDS LIFE TO YOUR YEARS

Have you noticed that when you get tense or feel pressure, you stop breathing? Or at least you stop breathing normally? You may not even realize it when it's happening, but it commonly occurs during arguments, in near-miss traffic mishaps, when making a mistake on the basketball court, when an angry customer is in your face explaining how you can't do anything right, and in hundreds of other scenarios throughout the course of your day that create tension. But without breathing at all, or when breathing improperly, your quality of thinking and performance can quickly shift from bad to worse, especially as you tense up, making you more prone to ineffective responses to the provocation. This is why in sports performance there's an essential adage: Control the mind and you control the breath; control your breath and you control your body; control your body and you control the performance. Here's why that's important: The breath brings oxygen to the brain, which helps you think clearly, and when you exhale deeply, you rid yourself of tension. Thus, the breath will bring you into the present moment and help you maximize that moment; in fact, it adds life to your moments.

When you need energy, focus on the inhalation. When you need to relax, focus on the exhalation. Good breath is the start of good rhythm. If you're not controlling your breathing, you can't control yourself. And while the adage is widely used in athletics, it applies to elevating the excellence of one's performance in any endeavor. In chapters three and four I first introduced a box breathing technique I taught to Joe and to Peter, the soon-to-turn-pro athlete, and I'll outline that specific routine and more in this chapter. While the breathing technique I'll share is only one of many effective routines, and I will describe through my personal experience how it has benefited me, I encourage you to research and try the techniques you find most useful in your own life.

◎ **BullsEYE Bullet:** Adding years to one's life without adding life to one's years mostly prolongs the mundaneness of one's existence.

AN *EYE* OPENER: MAKING MUSCLE MEMORY WORK FOR YOU

Halfway through my inaugural coaching Zoom with a new athlete client, "Troy," the conversation for how to improve his performance proceeded as thus:

Me: Do you know how to breathe?
Troy: Well, I've lived to be twenty-three years old so I guess I must be doing something right.

INTENTIONAL BREATHING ADDS LIFE TO YOUR YEARS

Me: Let me clarify: Do you know the importance of *intentional* breathing, and do you engage in any structured breathing exercises?

Troy: I obviously breathe deeper when I'm working out and breathe slower when sleeping, but I don't do anything deliberate or structured—just what comes naturally to fit the situation I'm in.

Me: You mentioned earlier that staying calm and thinking clearly under pressure was something you struggled with, especially when you turn the ball over or the opposing crowd is screaming when you're at the free throw line. We can feel the same type of pressure in business when dealing with an angry customer, having a tough accountability conversation with an employee, or even when we're cut off in traffic, and the principles of intentional breathing help in each of those situations. It slows you down, helps you think clearly, reduces tension, and puts you in the moment so you can more effectively deal with what is and is not stress over what just happened or what might happen next. Do you see how that can benefit you not just on the court but before giving a speech, taking a big exam, or arguing with an opposing player and more?

Troy: One hundred percent. But I would guess that it's hard to think of breathing intentionally in those situations, in the heat of the moment, precisely because they are pressure situations and your emotional triggers are pulled, so how do you fix that?

Me: One way is by doing the techniques as part of your daily routine, so it becomes natural for you, and you don't have to think about it. In fact, after a while, you won't even realize you're doing it, but your muscle memory from the breathing routines will have kicked in and you'll be doing it nonetheless.

Troy: Is this like meditation? Because I've done some of that.

Me: The objectives are similar: to get you in the moment, bring oxygen to the brain, reduce tension, and more. And my first breathing routine of the day is done before I get out of bed. It lasts around two and a half minutes, and then I segue right into another two-and-a-half-minute meditation routine, during which I bring my mind back to my breathing. Doing so conditions my mind early in the day to return to the present moment quickly after it wanders and begins focusing on what it can't control—what has already happened or will happen.

Troy: How long have you been doing this routine and how did you figure it out?

Me: I started working more on breathing back when I became a martial artist, and while there are numerous routines you can do and that I've studied that are beneficial, I learned this box breathing routine from Navy SEALs.

◎ **BullsEYE Bullet:** If you buy into the principle that how you do anything is how you do everything, then paying attention to something you do 23,000 times a day without really thinking about it warrants some thinking about.

SIX THOUGHTS, FACTS, AND STRATEGIES ABOUT INTENTIONAL BREATHING

1. When most people tense up or feel pressure, they stop breathing properly and can't think as clearly. This leads to poor decisions, inaction, overreaction, or other mistakes. Unhealthy tension is an enemy of performance. It can cause you to overtry, overthink, overreact, or become immobile.
2. You get 18 percent more oxygen into your body breathing in through your nose by boosting nitric oxide sixfold.[16, 17] Breathing in through the mouth is never as effective or healthy. In fact, if you breathe in through your mouth, oral bacteria multiplies faster and can even contribute to tooth decay, gum disease, and bad breath.
3. By being more intentional with inhaling through the nose while awake, you can condition your body to do likewise while sleeping. This can be especially helpful if you unconsciously inhale through your mouth while asleep. Exhaling through the mouth, on the other hand, is optimal for pushing out tension and more thoroughly purging carbon dioxide gas. Thus, when you inhale intentionally through the nose and exhale purposefully through the mouth, you position yourself for effective intentional breathing exercises like what is described in the next point.
4. Some Navy SEALs have an intentional breathing process they utilize to help clear their mind, stay in the moment, and remain calm: 4-4-6-2 × 6 reps × 6 sets. Like any discipline you wish to make a part of your nature so that it comes naturally, it's helpful to perform the technique regularly and consistently during your daily routine. Here's how it breaks down, as well as suggestions for how to weave in the various sets in subsequent points:

4—Inhale slowly through the nose for a count of four.

4—Hold the breath for four counts to keep you in the moment and you'll also benefit as it expands lung capacity.

6—Exhale slowly through the mouth for six counts to release tension and carbon dioxide.

2—Hold for two counts to stay in the moment and focus on beginning the next set.

×6—Do five more repetitions for a total of six repetitions.

×6—Repeat the process over again five more times throughout the day for a total of six sets.

You're certainly not limited to six repetitions or to six sets; if you're rolling and enjoying the benefits, keep rolling! These numbers provide enough repetition to bring an optimal benefit in the moment as well as to enable you to weave an intentional breathing discipline into your nature, over time. There may be days when you only do two sets, but that's still a big win over doing none. In other instances, such as when you're preparing to address a stressful situation, or after a near miss in traffic, even one or two deep breaths can calm you and help you think clearly. By making 4-4-6-2 × 6 × 6 the goal, you have something specific and effective to aspire to daily and to hold yourself accountable for at day's end.

5. Transitioning from intentional breathing to minutes of meditation is an add-on option to augment your conditioning to stay calm and in the moment during the day, especially before getting out of bed. As I mentioned to Troy during our coaching session at the opening of this chapter, you can then expand the breathing set into minutes of meditation simply by continuing the process.

The key to this brand of meditation is to focus on the breath. When your mind wanders, bring it back to the breath without judging it. Not only will this relax and center you, but you'll also become more aware of how often your mind is all over the place. By continually bringing your mind back to the breath when your mind wanders, you also develop the discipline to redirect your mind during your normal daily activities when it gets scattered and return it to being in the moment and focusing on what matters most. This is another example of a healthy habit becoming part of your nature when you do it so often that you no longer have to think about doing it at all.

6. Intentional breathing, which expands your lung capacity and improves respiratory health, is even more important when you realize you will lose some of your lung capacity from thirty to fifty years old, and more as you grow beyond that age.[18] Lung capacity can affect your energy, stamina, and overall well-being.

MY *PEAK:* STACK THE HABIT

The thought of squeezing six sets of intentional breathing into your already hectic day may strike you as being unreasonable or unrealistic. It did for me when I first learned the technique and the recommended frequency. To make it work I employed a discipline known as "stacking" or "layering" a habit. Here's how that works: take an existing habit, something that is part of your fixed routine, and add one of the breathing sets to it.

Here's an example for how it worked for me:

Set one
Knowing that until the day I'm no longer alive on this earth I will wake up each morning, this seemed like a simple place to layer the first set. Before getting out of bed, I do the first set of 4-4-6-2 × 6. It puts me in

the moment, oxygenates my body, and releases tension before I start my day; not a bad way to begin and stack a quick win before your feet hit the floor!

Set two
After finishing my morning hydration and grooming routine, I go to my recliner in the living room to begin my morning mindset routine—this is where I "take ten for mindset mastery." I layer my second set before beginning the routine, which puts me in an optimal state to get the most out of what I'm preparing to read, review, and learn.

Set three
Five days per week I commute to work, so early on during the commute, this is another natural habit to layer with 4-4-6-2 × 6. On the weekends when I don't commute, I do the set when I perform my early morning yard walk after my mindset routine, when I clear my head with fresh air and check out our flowers and vegetable and herb garden and take a moment to admire the Santa Monica Mountains in our backyard.

Set four
When at my office, I don't leave for lunch but take an hour away from all screen time to sit and think with a notepad and record ideas. I put my desk phone on "Do Not Disturb," close my office door, and move to a chair that is stationed on the other side of my office in front of the window facing the mountains. When I'm settled in, I pick up my legal pad in preparation for letting the right side of my brain have space to do its thing and get creative. Here I am prone to outline podcast topics, book chapters, marketing ideas, and more. Before I begin to pencil out ideas in my "thinking chair," I do my fourth breathing set,

which clears my mind and sets the tone for an in-the-moment hour of productive brainwork.

Set five
I do this breathing set during my commute back home after work and before a workout on the days I'm not at work.

Set six
As I retire for the evening, while lying in bed, I do the sixth breathing set, which helps me fall asleep as it slows my breathing and releases tension. There are many nights I don't make it through the six repetitions before I'm asleep.

Naturally we all have different schedules and routines, so my goal in sharing this is to get you to see how feasible it is to layer this habit with something you do on a regular basis just as I did, and how you can adjust it on the days when your routine isn't quite the same—in my case it's a weekend—and still find a way to execute the discipline rather than coming up with a reason why it's too hard or inconvenient.

🎯 **BullsEYE Bullet:** Adding life to your years starts with how you choose to think and feel and what you choose to do. Intentional breathing lends an assist in all three situations. Make it part of your nature.

TAKE ⑤ RAPID REVIEW AND ACTION STEPS

1. Consider a stressful work situation where breathing slowly and deeply can help center you and elicit a more measured and effective response to the provocation. Perhaps it's before interviewing a candidate or having a tough-love accountability conversation with a team member? Prior to going in to close a deal? In the moment or two before you get up to do your presentation at the meeting?
2. Do the same for situations you encounter away from work. Identify these areas up front, and intentional breathing becomes something to go to so you can still elevate your excellence, even when things get difficult.
3. Do you have aspects within your daily routines where you can layer a 4-4-6-2 × 6 set?
4. What can you substitute on the days that aren't as routine—like your day off—so you can still complete the discipline?
5. Consider the value of extending your first 4-4-6-2 × 6 set into a couple minutes of meditation before you get out of bed each morning to compound the benefits of beginning each day well and stacking multiple wins before your feet even hit the ground!

Chapter Ten

MASTERFUL SLEEPING ADDS YEARS TO YOUR LIFE

I never sleep!" snapped a high-level professional athlete to me in his text response after I asked him if he paid attention to mastering this essential discipline for peak performance. I had also suggested that he listen to episode #390, "Sleep Well, Perform Well, Live Well," of my podcast *The Game Changer Life*. His remark that he never slept was not a complaint, however, but rather a boast, indicating that between his vast business interests and dedicating himself rigorously to his professional craft, sleep was unimportant, secondary, something for "the weak" or lazy.

My response was simple: "If you never sleep, then please give that episode a listen, for the sake of your own health and for your family. You can tell me I'm full of it afterwards if it doesn't make sense or help you improve. But maybe at least take twentyish minutes to see what's up and possibly change your life. I never used to sleep either, and I bragged about it, but I had to change that. I don't oversleep, but I sleep enough and I sleep well; and I do so consistently, regardless of the time zone

I'm in—anywhere in the world. When I lie down in bed, I'm out in two minutes or less. And I'm in better health and have more energy and daily focus in my sixties than I did in my thirties."

While intentional breathing adds life to your years, and this chapter on sleep will show how undersleeping can subtract years from your life, you'll also see that inadequate sleep negatively impacts the quality of your years. Without enough quality sleep—sleeping well for seven to nine hours per night—you can suffer loss of memory, lack of emotional control, irritability, trouble making decisions or solving problems, scattered focus, low creativity levels, brain disease, and more. These conditions affect your mental health, relationships, mood, performance, and overall well-being. In other words, they greatly inhibit your ability to elevate your excellence in any vital life arena. And since you spend roughly one-third of your life sleeping, or at least trying to sleep, isn't it worth taking the time to learn more about how to do this ordinary task extraordinarily well?

> **BullsEYE Bullet:** Sleeping well is a daily catalyst for the effective application of "how you do anything is how you do everything." It's fair to say that the first win you stack in a day is upon waking after a great night's sleep.

AN *EYE* OPENER: A FOOLISH BOAST

As I mentioned to my professional athlete friend in this chapter's second paragraph, I used to boast about being able to get by with very little sleep because I saw it as an ally in my endeavor to overachieve in any job I had. After all, with less time spent asleep, I could work more and engage in additional activities to help me become more successful, get ahead of the competition, and get the most out of life. I was fond of repeating the adage, "I'll sleep when I'm dead." After taking renowned sleep scientist Matthew Walker's online course on sleep and reading his book, *Why We Sleep*, I became convinced that I would indeed sleep when I was dead, and that I would likely be dead earlier than necessary based on my miserly sleep habits.

Dr. Walker's information also alerted me to the reality that my performance while awake was greatly impacted by how well I slept the night before; that while I was considered successful in my work, my results were in spite of being chronically underslept and not because of it. As I practiced better sleep principles like I share in this chapter, and I began teaching them to the underslept athletes and business clients I worked with, their testimonials and progress further encouraged me to get the word out. Three decades ago, when I began writing books and teaching seminars, I never foresaw including a chapter or teaching sections on mastering the art of sleep. But it is so essential to elevating your excellence in all your vital life arenas, especially your health, that I'd be remiss and irresponsible for not sharing it. It has changed my life, and I hope it does for you and those you care about as well.

◉ **BullsEYE Bullet:** You don't actually "get up on the wrong side of the bed." That tone gets set long before you even go to bed and during the time you spend there. By the time you get up on either side of the bed, it's too late; your excellence that day has been largely determined.

ELEVEN TERMS TO SET THE STAGE

As I studied sleep from Dr. Matthew Walker's course and book, it broadened my vocabulary as I became familiar with scientific terms and the names of various parts of the brain. It can get a bit confusing, so I'm going to introduce eleven terms here that you may or may not be familiar with, to lay a foundation of basic understanding for how these will set the stage for better comprehension as the chapter progresses. Don't blame me for suddenly sounding academic: I didn't name this stuff; I'm just trying to explain it!

Sleep chronotype
Nine genes in your body determine whether you are a morning lark (a morning person), a night owl (a night person), or somewhere in between. This will change as you age from being a toddler to a teen to an adult, and it may change over again as you begin to age into your twilight years. It can also be "rewired" over time in different time zones, or when you go from working a day shift to a late-night shift. What's important is to be aware of where you're at now in your current life stage.

Circadian rhythm
Your circadian rhythm is an internal clock that winds your body up and down based on your sleep chronotype. It helps you be and stay awake when it's time to be awake and to get to sleep at the appropriate time as well.

Suprachiasmatic nucleus (SCN)
Your SCN is housed in the anterior hypothalamus of the brain and helps control your circadian rhythm. It is also responsible for releasing melatonin to help you sleep. As the surroundings and environment you're in darken, melatonin is released, and you begin to get sleepy. If you're in a bright room or taking in blue light from electronic devices in the evening when you're within range of your bedtime, your SCN believes it's still supposed to be daytime and doesn't release the melatonin as it's designed to do, making it harder to become sleepy.

Melatonin

Melatonin is a natural hormone that helps put you to sleep and is released by your SCN as the light diminishes. It doesn't affect the quality or length of your sleep in your younger years as much as when you age. As you age, your body releases less melatonin and you may need supplements. However, if you can't get to sleep in the first place, then you're not going to sleep well enough or long enough anyhow, so in this respect, melatonin plays an important aspect in helping you master the art of great sleep.

Adenosine

Adenosine is a natural compound that builds up on the brain throughout the course of the day to create sleep pressure at night to help you sleep. As you sleep, the brain scrubs off the adenosine so that when you awaken, you feel refreshed. When you are underslept, adenosine—acting as sleep pressure—remains on the brain, making you feel more tired. The purpose of caffeine is to block the adenosine receptors. When this occurs, the adenosine builds up but is blocked from taking effect. When the caffeine wears off, the buildup of adenosine comes crashing down, making you feel tired.

Prefrontal cortex

This acts as the CEO of the brain and restores healthy connections with other brain aspects as you sleep deep enough and long enough.

Amygdala

This small, almond-shaped structure inside your brain is part of your limbic system that comprises the emotional part of the brain. With deep, long sleep, its healthy connections with the prefrontal cortex are restored so your emotions are more stable the next day, and you're also better able to accurately discern the emotions of others. Thus, when you are deprived of sleep, you can become more easily irritable, angry, and emotionally volatile overall.

Hippocampus
This aspect of the brain acts as your memory storage—a hard drive of sorts—and during sleep that's deep and long enough, it downloads memories from your short- to long-term memory. This is why being sleep deprived can cause an impaired recall of details and other memories.

Non-REM (non-rapid eye movement) sleep
These are the early stages of sleep, of which there are four in total. At stages three and four, the prefrontal cortex repairs connections with the amygdala, and your hippocampus begins to download short-term to long-term memories.

REM (rapid-eye movement) sleep
REM sleep is when you dream, which is an essential aspect of masterful sleep. REM sleep normally comes ninety minutes into non-REM sleep and recycles in and out every ninety minutes until you awaken. The first stage is normally ten minutes, and the final is for roughly an hour and is thus the most beneficial segment.

During REM sleep, parts of your brain interact with the others at a level they can't at any other time. REM sleep is essential for creativity, and its benefits are often evident after waking up with an answer, idea, or solution you had been looking for and needed to "sleep on." This level of sleep is where your brain can give you those "Eureka!" moments. The danger is that when you're underslept, you're missing out on the longest and most beneficial period of REM sleep, which impairs your creativity.

Glymphatic system

This is the brain's "sewage system" that removes a harmful buildup of amyloid proteins when you're in stages three and four of non-REM sleep. If you don't get into a deep enough sleep, the glymphatic system isn't activated and these proteins accumulate, potentially causing the brain harm over time. So, if you're one who boasts that you "never sleep," perhaps considering the growing buildup of these proteins on your brain should motivate you to do better.

◎ **BullsEYE Bullet:** If you spend roughly one-third of your life asleep, and if the quality of your sleep impacts the quality of your waking hours, isn't it time you put in the work to excel at this essential discipline if you don't already?

FIFTEEN TIPS FOR BETTER SLEEP

One of the recurring themes of this book is that "great performance at anything begins before it begins," and getting great sleep is no exception. You must set yourself up for success with the right decisions, disciplines, and routines leading up to your bedtime. Following are a variety of tips to improve the length and quality of your sleep before it's time to sleep—and while you sleep. The more of these you pay attention to or execute, the better your sleep and your waking performance becomes. While I've studied sleep science, I'm no expert on it, and what I'm sharing are techniques I've learned, applied, and benefitted from personally. I encourage you to do your own research and apply what best fits your own liking and lifestyle.

Don't eat or snack close to bedtime

Cutting off food two to three hours before bedtime is ideal. Otherwise, just about the time you want your body to wind down and get to sleep, you put it to work breaking down and processing food. Especially avoid sugary foods that spike your bloodstream and heighten your level of alertness close to bedtime. This not only impairs your sleep but impacts your weight.

Minimize caffeine intake in the afternoon and evening

Caffeine blocks the adenosine receptors in your brain and doesn't allow the sleep pressure to take effect and make you sleepy. Keep in mind that 50 percent of caffeine remains in your system after six hours, and another 25 percent remains for six additional hours. Considering points one and three in this tip section, it's easy to see how a heavy late-night meal, with a caffeinated beverage, topped off with dessert and alcohol, can be devastating to getting great sleep. The heavy meal may make you drowsy and help put you to sleep, but you're unlikely to sleep deeply or long enough to feel well rested and energized in the morning.

Avoid alcohol within a couple hours of bedtime

While alcohol makes you drowsy, it doesn't help you sleep deeply or long. In fact, it attacks your nervous system and makes it aware that "something isn't right," which creates a higher level of alertness and agitation, so, despite dozing off, you're less likely to sleep deeply or uninterrupted.

Get dark

If your surroundings are too light, your SCN won't release the melatonin that makes you sleepy. If you're on the phone, computer, or watching television prior to bed, all of this affects your SCN and melatonin release. Darken your room and wear blue-light-blocker glasses at night to eliminate the effect of "device" light and allow the melatonin to be released. These glasses are common, inexpensive, and can easily be purchased online.

Get cool
Your body temperature drops when you sleep, so it helps if the room is already chilled and stays cool for the duration of your slumber. Sixty-seven degrees is optimal. You can also wear fewer clothes to bed, if any at all, to keep your body cooler.

Get a melatonin boost
To help fall asleep, take a melatonin supplement one hour before bedtime. Don't take more than prescribed amounts or you can inhibit the natural melatonin released by your brain. And while melatonin may not help as much with the quality and length of your sleep, it at least helps put you to sleep in the first place. And remember, as previously mentioned, that as you grow older, your body may produce less melatonin naturally, and a supplement can be even more beneficial. Be aware also that melatonin is among supplements unregulated by the FDA, which is why it's important to take only what is prescribed.

Use aloe vera gel
Apply aloe vera gel to your face and torso before going to bed. Not only is this good for your skin, but it is cooling and can help trick your body into thinking it should be dialing down and going to sleep as the temperature drops.

Breathe!
Do the 4-4-6-2 × 6 breathing technique soon after you go to bed to relax your body, slow your breathing, and trick your brain into thinking it should be asleep. You can repeat this sequence multiple times until you

get to sleep. As mentioned in chapter nine, this is an easy and natural place to layer one of your sets for this breathing exercise.

Be selective
Only use your bed for intimacy and sleep. This trains your brain that when you're in bed, you're there to do one or the other, maybe both, but nothing else! This means you don't read or watch television in bed. And certainly, don't complicate great sleep further by snacking in bed while you watch television, sipping brandy, and taking in blue light while texting on your phone!

Get up!
If you can't fall asleep, don't just lie there waiting to doze off. Just as you don't sit at the kitchen table waiting until you're hungry, don't lie in bed if you can't sleep, simply waiting until you're sleepy. Following up on the prior point, this is about training your brain that a bed is for sleep. So, get up, and go to a chair, and do things that make you sleepy: read (with dim light), breathe, meditate, and the like. Then when you feel sleepy, come back to bed.

Power naps
Whenever possible, avoid naps that last longer than twenty minutes. Why? Napping too long removes too much sleep pressure—adenosine—from your brain that will make it tougher to sleep later. It also throws off your circadian rhythm—your twenty-four-hour biological clock.

Don't nap late
Try not to take a nap of any kind past 4 PM. Naturally, this will vary according to your work schedule, but if your days progress within standard norms regarding time, napping past four o'clock is likely too close

to sleep time and will make it unlikely you sleep deeply enough to fall into the optimal REM sleep state. Since napping late makes you more freshly rested, and the sleep pressure of adenosine is scrubbed off while you nap, getting into a deep enough sleep for prolonged periods is more challenging. It can cause you to wake up throughout the night or become fully awake too early and disrupt your optimal daily rhythm.

Sleep early on long flights
If you're on an international or otherwise several-hour flight across multiple time zones, sleep on the early leg of the flight so that when you land, you're better able to get into the rhythm of your new location. Get your brain used to where you're going by setting your watch early in the flight and toughing out the first day in your new location, resisting the temptation to go to bed and rest upon arrival (unless it is your normal sleep time). If you can stay awake until whatever your normal bedtime would be where you've arrived, you'll more quickly adjust your circadian rhythm to its new location, and it'll minimize the effect of the time change the remainder of your stay.

The right exercise
If you exercise before you sleep, light exercise is best, and light stretching can help, as it relaxes you and gets tension out of your muscles. However, strenuous exercise close to bedtime can heat up your organs and body and make it more difficult to wind down and sleep, especially if you eat or drink a pre- or post-workout snack that your body must work to break down and process.

Warm bath
While at first it may sound counterintuitive, taking a warm bath before bed helps sleep. This is because the water temperature makes the blood

rise to the top of your skin, which evacuates the heat and makes your body temperature cooler when you get out of the bath.

Without a doubt, some of these tips may not appeal to you or work for you based on the unique circumstances of your lifestyle. But the good news is that you won't need to implement any great number of them to quickly see improvement in the quality of your sleep. Experiment and find those that bring you the best result. Customize your own "master the discipline of great sleep" plan to elevate your own excellence by using these suggestions and others like them as a buffet of possibilities you can pick from and make work for you.

◎ **BullsEYE Bullet:** Not everything will work for you, but your results won't change for you until you change something.

MY *PEAK:* AN UNEXPECTED BONUS

In my work I have the pleasure of personally coaching, sometimes in person but mostly by Zoom meetings, athletes and business professionals from all over the world and in multiple areas of expertise. During a session with "Tom," a successful entrepreneur, we were discussing some of his personal and professional objectives, some of which were to:

- focus more on what matters most during the day;
- garner higher levels of mental and physical energy so that he didn't fizzle prematurely at day's end;
- improve his creativity levels and ability to make big decisions faster.

Upon further discussion, it became clear that his current inability to optimize his daily performance in these areas was related to his erratic sleep habits: not getting enough sleep and not sleeping well when he did sleep. Thus, our coaching session took a different direction than he had expected, as we discussed nothing of the issues he was endeavoring to improve, and we focused instead on a single core issue that would improve them all: mastering effective sleep disciplines. In fact, our entire hour was invested to this end.

When we met for a one-month follow-up and accountability session, he was as excited as I'd ever seen anyone on a coaching session, as he discussed how quickly the sleep disciplines worked for him once he applied them, and how they had positively elevated his excellence in every area of concern we had resolved to improve. But he wasn't finished. He said that since he had also started eating his final meal an hour earlier and had eliminated his habitual late-night sugary snacks, he'd lost eight pounds in the thirty days since we'd last visited. This is the power of addressing core issues like a lack of great sleep, rather than trying to treat the symptoms that the unresolved underlying issues will continue to produce.

BullsEYE Bullet: "There are a thousand hacking at the branches of evil to one who is striking at the root."[19]

—Henry David Thoreau

ELEVATE YOUR EXCELLENCE

> **TAKE 5 RAPID REVIEW AND ACTION STEPS**
>
> 1. List any aspects about your performance or life overall that you believe are inhibited by being underslept, or by sleeping poorly when you do sleep, that are hurting your ability to elevate your excellence during your waking hours:
>   - Lack of emotional control
>   - Poor memory
>   - Trouble making decisions or being creative
>   - A scattered focus
>   - Low or erratic energy levels
>   - Something else
> 2. Which of the listed suggestions for better sleep that this chapter reinforces and encourages do you currently include in your routine?
> 3. Are late-night meals or snacking habitual for you? Do you struggle with weight control? Could this be a contributing factor?
> 4. Remember that you'll never be 100 percent on track with your sleep disciplines all the time. You're human. Life gets in the way, and circumstances beyond your control can knock you off track. Thus, endeavor to be more aware of what "the right track" looks like so that when you do get off track, you recognize it faster and make a quicker course correction.
> 5. Which of the sleep tips are practical for you? You can start implementing them today or tonight!

Chapter Eleven
CHALLENGE YOURSELF

The general manager I was having a coaching conversation with wasn't sure at first where I was going in that conversation after my first sentence, but it quickly sank in and resonated in a big way. And what I said to him applies equally to people in any field:

> One of the biggest problems I see holding you back is that you do what's required of you. Sometimes you even do more than is required. But you don't do *all you can*. You underchallenge yourself. In order to elevate your excellence and test higher personal limits, you've got to answer the question 'How much is enough?' with 'All I can,' and do so every time, with whatever you're doing. I want us to work on conditioning your conscience so that when you're doing less than you can, you call yourself out with accountability, then call yourself up to a higher level of performance. Doing this consistently won't just change your career, it will change your life.

I would strongly suggest that the number one thing holding most well-intentioned people back from dreaming big enough, or from achieving even the modest dreams they have, is their unhealthy, baseline, mostly small thinking. Many of them have the skills, knowledge, and talent to get what they want or do better than they have previously imagined, but their thinking gets in the way. They've projected some of this unhealthy thinking upon themselves, and they've let others predict some for them, giving them a negative label to live down to. This sort of "put myself in a box" or "buy into the box I'm put into" mindset creates limiting beliefs, a poor self-image, deflated self-esteem, and depleted self-confidence. The good news is that challenging yourself isn't a decision you have to wait for anyone else to make for you; it's a choice you can make in a split second and then follow up with action.

In truth, despite what others say or think about us, no one else has the power to inflict any fenced-in conditions on us; but, even though they don't have that wherewithal, we grant it to them nonetheless by buying into their judgments and biases against us, which can eventually shape our self-image with statements such as:

"Know your place."
"Just go with the flow."
"You're already doing great so why are you working so hard?"
"That kind of life isn't for people like us."
"You know you're going to find a way to mess it up again."
"You're already number one so just bask and enjoy it."
"Why risk it?"
"It'll make you uncomfortable."

This litany of "mold you for mediocrity" misery could go on for several more paragraphs.

CHALLENGE YOURSELF

What lies about your abilities, your potential, or your future have you manufactured about yourself or bought into from others that are stopping you from elevating your excellence? Or from making changes, improving routines, strengthening disciplines, competing daily with your former self, and striving to live your best life daily? Do you really want to stay in that space, or is it just safer and more comfortable for you to be there? Are you allowing your negatively biased brain to beat down your once hungrier heart?

If you've been underchallenging yourself and settling for what's good enough, or even for what's great, and it's stopping you from what's *best*, it's time to reshape your thinking. My own belief is that if you've started to embrace and apply even a small number of the action steps in the book thus far, and you're in the process of elevating your personal and performance excellence, then you have strengthened—or perhaps even rebuilt—a personal performance foundation from which you can reach for what's going to truly challenge you, inspire you, and change your life for the better. I'm not saying it'll be easy, and it surely won't be comfortable, but it will be worth every bit of effort you expend. After all, it's all right to aim high if you have plenty of ammunition. And some of the best ammunition in pursuit of your best goals is the healthy thinking that influences improved behaviors and creates elevated excellence.

Oppositely, if you're already a big-thinking person who routinely challenges yourself but don't want to plateau or regress—or maybe it's been a while since you've taken the big swing and really gone for something that scared you—it's time for you to refocus, recommit, and re-challenge yourself to not settle for less than what you were designed to become and to do. The moment, the day, the life you have in front of you isn't a dress rehearsal. There are no redos. If it's time to challenge yourself at a higher level, this chapter should be a good read for you.

◎ **BullsEYE Bullet:** There are two ways to miss the mark when living your life: trying to go too far and falling short, or choosing not to go far enough and staying put. If I'm going to fail, it'll be by trying to go too far because it's only in trying to go too far that I'll ever find out how far I can go. I won't discover how far I can go by deciding not to go far enough. And neither will you.

AN *EYE* OPENER: THE "110 PERCENT" TOMORROW LIE

In my first sales management job, my team and I had just finished a record month. I hadn't yet learned how to survive success and overcome the pitfalls of complacency that often accompany prosperity. My team and I started the first four days of the next month in neutral, creating few sales and continuing to regale our numbers from the month before. We were in danger of letting our pats on the back turn into a massage and a victory lap become a marathon, when the owner called me into his office.

Boss: Anderson, what happened yesterday?

Me: It was an off day, and today is slow too, but we'll give 110 percent and make up for it tomorrow.

Boss: Anderson, there is no "110 percent tomorrow" BS. That's what losers say to excuse or rationalize their failure to execute today. There's just 100 percent each day, and if you don't give it all in a day, it's lost forever. Tomorrow could for sure be outstanding, but it won't make up for what you lost yesterday, or lose today, through your lack of focus, effort, or your indifference.

CHALLENGE YOURSELF

Each day has got to stand on its own. So, lose that weaker-than-worm-whiz mindset that you can slack today and make up ground later. Wake up, son, because you can't! That time and those opportunities you missed are gone forever. Last month ended four nights ago. Get your a** back to work, and prove yourself again this month. Show me I've got the right guy in this job.

Needless to say, my boss's message came across loud and clear and was one of the most helpful lessons I ever learned to help me elevate my excellence and survive success by keeping a consistently hungry mindset. I applied it broadly throughout my life: to dates with my wife, dinners with my family, workouts in the gym and at the dojo, and more. It has helped me continue to challenge myself and stay in the moment—to not visit or dwell in the past for self-congratulatory applause, or to shift down and go through the motions with any task, but to bring all that I could every day, and then the next day, and the next, until it became part of my nature. I learned that if you're not all in every day, you're not really in at all.

BullsEYE Bullet: "Success isn't owned. It's leased, and rent is due every day."[20]

—J.J. Watt

EIGHT TIPS TO TAP THE POWER OF CHALLENGING YOURSELF

Following are eight insights and strategies to leverage the power of challenging yourself and testing your limits.

Better, More, More Often

Challenging yourself isn't always about doing something completely new or different. The most obvious and effective place to start is by taking the nonnegotiable behaviors and activities you engage in daily and learning to do them better. Then when you're doing them better, you'll have the desire and confidence to do more of them. And when the results of doing more of the best things better manifest, and you enjoy those results, you naturally progress to improve your consistency by doing them more often. The "better, more, more often" strategy is the low-hanging fruit to challenging yourself because you're building it on a foundation of familiarity and strength that exists already.

Which essential productive behaviors and activities that you engage in will you commit to calling yourself out on and doing better, more, and more often? Rise to the challenge, do them, and elevate your excellence!

Incremental Gains Performed Consistently Compound Exponentially

Challenging yourself to elevate your excellence isn't about making quantum leaps in one fell swoop—doubling or tripling your goal just to make you uncomfortable enough to change, while at the same time possibly causing you to quickly check out of the goal mentally if it's taking too long or you encounter obstacles early. The fact is that incremental gains, performed consistently, compound exponentially into quantum gains.

The following illustration is not presented as a recommended method or system for working out. My goals are not to offend the sensibilities of personal trainers or "gym rats" reading these words, who, in their haste to take offense, may miss the point entirely. And that point is to simply

CHALLENGE YOURSELF

use this as an example to show you the power of incremental gains performed consistently.

If you've mastered a simple workout program where you do five sets of twenty push-ups daily and try to double the amount to five sets of forty overnight, you'd likely find by the third set that you'd taken on more than you can handle at once. And rather than challenge yourself, you'd walk away discouraged, failing to stack a win.

But, if you chose to make jumps in increments of reasonable percentages—10 percent at a time, for example—you'd likely complete all five sets performing twenty-two reps per set, or at least come close. This practice of going beyond what you've currently mastered and are comfortable with completely qualifies as "calling yourself out." It's also calling yourself up to a point beyond your current mastery level. And in this example, while you're only increasing your productive activities by two per set, think of it instead in terms of percentages—10 percent—which is a significant increase in productive activities at one time. In a short while, the twenty-two push-ups per set would likely feel routine and less challenging and be a candidate for another modest 10 percent increase, up to twenty-four. Repeat it again in a short while and you'd be at twenty-six repetitions, a 30 percent increase over your original twenty push-ups.

Now imagine you were also increasing other important disciplines with modest bumps at the same time: perhaps the number of sales-prospecting calls you make at work, or the number of pages you read in a book each evening, and the like. You'd be constantly stacking wins, building confidence, and improving your mental, physical, and work performance, and, in due time, racking up substantial performance increases that would have seemed impossible had you tried to jump straight to that higher amount at the outset in the name of challenging yourself, but without having a solid enough foundation of confidence and competence to meet the challenge or sustain the performance. Look at challenging yourself as anything you're doing above and beyond what you're currently comfortably doing, not necessarily as a super-stretch goal to stir your passions momentarily, but something that you're likely to fail to achieve or sustain by attempting it in one large leap.

Stretch More from Your Areas of Personal Strengths

In areas where you have significant personal strengths, you will likely be able to set higher percentage increases than what I used in the prior example. This is because you would have already established a foundation of confidence and expertise and will find it easier to go from good to great than from miserable to mediocre in areas where you are not as gifted. Keep your options open when challenging yourself. You don't need to apply the same percentage increases in all your life disciplines because you're not likely equally gifted in each discipline.

Change and Challenge Before You Have To

Don't wait until you've plateaued or are in decline to begin challenging yourself! Frankly, being in a rut or in decline (sloping downward) may be evidence you stopped challenging yourself some time ago and have gotten comfortable with living life in a maintenance mode that preceded your currently unhappy state. Though it may initially seem counterintuitive, challenging yourself and elevating your excellence while you're doing the best you've ever done is highly impactful, as it helps you survive success and pull yourself forward from the natural drift towards stagnations and complacency when you're doing well. Human beings don't naturally continue to move forward when they're winning—they normally slide backward—so continually challenging yourself can offset that natural tendency and condition you have to become unnatural in a very productive way!

Get Comfortable Being Uncomfortable

Challenging yourself creates discomfort, if even in a slight way, which is essential to growth, as it's implausible to think you can possibly grow anything other than your waistline or list of excuses for why you're not improving while you're frozen in a comfort zone or calcified in a mold. So, the more you challenge yourself, the more you'll become comfortable being uncomfortable, which is an essential ally to elevating your excellence in all life's vital arenas throughout the course of your lifetime. Make being uncomfortable part of your nature! It helps you feel alive, alert, energized, and confident. It's a key ally to stacking wins throughout the day and being better today than you were the day, week, or month before.

Expand Your Capacity to Produce

I first read about the connection between how one's ability to create production is limited by one's capacity to produce in Stephen R. Covey's book *The 7 Habits of Highly Effective People* decades ago. It's a lesson that stuck with me because of its simplicity and unimpeachable wisdom. You can't make withdrawals from a performance bank where you haven't made deposits in terms of elevating your skills; knowledge; habits; attitudes; or spiritual, mental, physical, or emotional well-being; any more than you can clear checks you write on deficient bank balances.

In terms of production, if all you've ever done is X, and you want to elevate your performance to Y or Z, you'll need to have or build a capacity that enables those gains. So, while you should challenge yourself incrementally and in multiple areas of your life simultaneously, you must also fortify yourself with the growth in those areas that will support your continual stretching. To put it another way, don't just work on your performance, work on you! Your performance will improve when you do. And you'll improve when you work intentionally on yourself.

Hold Yourself Accountable

It's become almost cliché to hear people resolve, "I'll hold myself more accountable." But what exactly does that mean, and how do you pull it off? I touched on this back in chapter four and want to expand in greater detail here.

Essentially there are three steps to follow to hold oneself accountable daily, and the first begins with daily clarity, without which daily accountability can't credibly happen.

Daily clarity

The night before, establish your daily priorities for the upcoming day and schedule them onto your calendar. Accountability is impossible without clarity because the question becomes "Accountable for what?" You must have a specific daily basis for accountability—a win-or-lose proposition regarding the most essential activities you must execute to move you closer to the ultimate outcomes you desire most.

Game film

Just as an athlete watches video of their performance to reinforce positives and correct errors, so must you. And while you won't have a literal movie reel to watch at day's end, you will have the priorities you established in the prior point to compare against what you actually accomplished. Notice in which areas you did well and ask yourself why. "Why was I successful?"

CHALLENGE YOURSELF

This is important because without being resolutely clear as to why you were successful, you're less likely to duplicate that success. What nonsense did you say no to so that you could accomplish that handful of best things? Did you follow processes more closely, start the day with more focus, walk away from unproductive people and situations, and return faster to what mattered most when you veered off track? Make note and incorporate those lessons into your next day's routine to duplicate your success.

But also notice where you fell short and failed to accomplish what you set out to do and ask yourself the same *why* questions. Take responsibility for what you could have controlled better, and weave those lessons into tomorrow's plan as well.

Plan tomorrow the night before

Accounting for the lessons you learned during your post-workday game filming, schedule tomorrow's priorities the night before and review them again in your morning routine so that when you enter your performance arena, you are laser locked on what matters most and ready to execute your way to elevated excellence throughout the day. Then repeat it day after day.

Begin Again More Intelligently

Whenever you venture to do more than you've done, you are disrupting your comfortable patterns and routines and can expect to make mistakes and find yourself off course. You're human. It happens. So, pick yourself up; don't beat yourself up. What will separate you from the masses who consider missteps a "sign" they should venture no further—and possibly also from the playbook of your former play-it-safe self—is developing the ability to catch yourself faster when you take a misstep and then get back on track. Notice why you got off track, accept responsibility for the aspects of the misfire you could have controlled, and do better going forward. As Henry Ford famously said, "Failure is only the opportunity to more intelligently begin again."[21]

The benefit of following a strong daily structure anchored by effective routines and rituals is that you'll be establishing a very clear daily road to follow. And much like traveling on a new, pothole-free superhighway, you'll recognize any drifting onto a bumpy road shoulder faster. The danger is to remain on that bumpy road shoulder long enough to become used to it and for it to feel normal, which is a form of complacency that invites ruts into your life. The more familiar you are with what the right course is, the faster you'll realize you're in unfamiliar territory and return to a structure of success. Incidentally, this discipline will help you run circles around the hordes of hapless folks bumbling through life who aren't even sure what their course is. In fact, many make it up as they go along daily.

◉ **BullsEYE Bullet:** By definition, *challenge* means "to make demands on." It doesn't say set unrealistic goals beyond what you're currently doing. The point is to extend yourself past what you're comfortably doing and thereby stack another win in your vertical climb to elevate your excellence.

MY *PEAK:* SEIZE WHAT ANOTHER SEES

Ideally, we will see or sense our inner greatness, recognize our uniqueness, continue to challenge ourselves, and resolve to let nothing stand in the way of higher aspirations. But oftentimes, for whatever reason, that's not the case, and that's where I found myself as a car salesman, sixty days into the business, at Parnell Chrysler Plymouth Jeep Eagle in Wichita

CHALLENGE YOURSELF

Falls, Texas. This dealership has long since moved locations after having been acquired by new owners, but that blacktop was my launching pad for an automotive retail career that not only changed my life financially but provided opportunities to grow and impact others beyond what I thought was possible when I took the job. It was the only job I could find at the time, and I'd just been turned down by their competitor, Alpha Dodge, where the manager told me he didn't think I had the inner fire to succeed in the automotive retail business.

As a twenty-something-year-old broke kid who skipped college, my biggest competitive edge was focus and drive. I wasn't thinking big or prioritizing growth at the time. I was consumed with "survival." I needed that one-thousand-dollar-per-month guaranteed draw against commissions to keep a stable place to live, to put gas in my clunker and bread on the table. Despite my long hours of hard work, I produced only average results in my first two months in the business. The dealership offered very little training, so to gain an edge I began investing in books on selling to improve my skills. I recall the first book I read on the topic was Tom Hopkins's *How to Master the Art of Selling*, and I soon progressed to Zig Ziglar's book, *See You at the Top*. I studied the product and practiced scripts in work downtime while others sat in their circle outside and smoked, complained, and argued about who would have to take the next customer.

Harold Parnell was the dealership's owner, and he had a habit of writing brief notes on paycheck stubs. Some were kind, and some were sarcastic, based on your performance. While I was a middle-of-the-pack performer at the start of my third month in the business, I read the note on my meager check from Harold one Friday that said, *"We're waiting for you to make your move. Show us you're number one."*

I had to do a double take to make sure I had the right paycheck, and the lean amount affirmed that indeed it was. But without exaggeration, those thirteen words of affirmation and belief helped change my life.

Sometimes you don't, or can't, see in yourself what others see because you're too close to it, or it's been buried beneath guilt, regret, low self-esteem, the embarrassment of past failures, or an inability to forgive yourself and move on from past flops. And because of that limited vision, you'd be unlikely to challenge yourself to more but would gladly settle instead for just getting by or maybe a little bit ahead. Harold spoke life into my spirit that day. He called me out and called me up. He saw in a future me success I couldn't see myself. His words created a mental shift in me, and I saw myself differently, and I began to act in accordance with that self-image to prove him right, soon thereafter going on a performance roll where I was top salesperson of the month for fifteen consecutive months before being offered a job as sales manager from the largest dealership group in the city.

While this chapter has been focused on stretching yourself, making yourself uncomfortable, and discovering your own greatness, I want to close it out by also encouraging you to challenge others. Call them out and call them up. Help them discover the inner greatness and uniqueness within them that they're too blind, brainwashed, or scared to see. Speak life into them as Harold did into me. You'll win and so will they.

◎ **BullsEYE Bullet:** "It's impossible to consistently behave in a manner inconsistent with how we see ourselves. We can do very few things in a positive way if we feel negative about ourselves."[22]

—Zig Ziglar

CHALLENGE YOURSELF

TAKE (5) RAPID REVIEW AND ACTION STEPS

1. Are there areas of your life where you've set goals *too* high in regards to the time you've given yourself to reach them, and have you subsequently mentally checked out of those goals or no longer realistically believe in reaching them? List any that apply.

2. In which areas of your personal growth, exercise, work routine, and more can you challenge yourself to simultaneously incrementally and consistently raise your performance, planting the seeds for exponential growth over time?

3. Which of the three aspects of holding yourself accountable daily do you do currently? What can you begin or improve? Remember: without daily accountability, most of your plans for improvement become simply a futile and intellectual exercise.

4. Are your routines structured enough so that you can catch yourself faster when you get off track? If not, what do you need to fine-tune so they are?

5. Overall, considering all of your life arenas, where have you gotten too comfortable? What will you do to change that? Where do you need to become comfortable being uncomfortable?

Chapter Twelve

ELEVATE YOURSELF AND OTHERS: WRITE THE BOOK

I never thought I was smart enough to write a book, and I've no doubt there are more than a modicum of readers of my works over the decades who would agree I was correct! After all, I didn't have an impressive formal education, and while I enjoyed and was better at English and literature classes in school than I was at math—that isn't saying much—what I did write, while it came easy to me, never seemed exceptional. I believe many people feel the same: that for whatever reason they don't have the "right stuff" to write much of anything, much less a book, whatever they think that right stuff happens to be. But they do have the right stuff because writing isn't about having technical skills—you can learn those skills or subcontract experts for that—it's about having a story to tell, lessons to relay, and experiences to share. And from that standpoint, everyone has the right stuff of a unique perspective and story to tell because no one has lived exactly how they've lived or had identical challenges and experiences over the course of their life.

There are plenteous benefits of writing that help you elevate your excellence in areas far removed from the writing itself that I'll present in this chapter. Even if you don't think you're a good writer, feel you have little to say worth writing, or perhaps you don't enjoy writing at all, writing in a journal or authoring a book will create an initial discomfort that can precede growth in many vital life arenas. If you will keep an open mind as you entertain the thoughts in the next few pages, you may discover an unexplored and previously unconsidered path to being your best you. And if you do enjoy writing, and you have always wanted to journal or create your own written work, or perhaps you have already, this chapter could be exactly what you've been waiting for to begin putting your ideas on paper, or to take the writing you already do and perform it with more purpose and excellence to maximize the benefits writing delivers. As you do so, I believe you'll discover, as have I and many others, that it's what you learn and become in the process of writing that compounds its value and elevates your life and, in many cases, the lives of others as well.

AN *EYE* OPENER: THE STORY WITHIN YOU

While I've personally enjoyed writing since grade school (it's not false modesty to admit I was good at little else in school), I'm aware it's not everyone's "thing." On the other hand, considering the number of people I've met in three decades of signing the books I've written for readers and in interacting with seminar attendees, it has astounded me how many of them tell me they have a book idea, or would like to write a book, but still never do. In fact, I've come to believe that everyone has a book in them, because everyone on Earth has traversed a journey that's unique and unlike exactly what anyone else has experienced. My belief that everyone has a book in them waiting to come out was validated when, during the COVID shutdowns of 2020, I posted a short "Write the Book" video on social media, encouraging viewers to use the downtime they had at their disposal to write a story, or their story, and in return received tenfold more enthusiastic comments than normal for a simple and incidental post.

And writing needn't be in depth or in book form to benefit the writer in multiple ways. Even a discipline that's as simple and brief as recording your thoughts daily in a gratitude journal can elevate your excellence in areas far beyond what I have room to discuss in this chapter. Thus, I'll present a sketch of the most obvious benefits, and how doing so can elevate your excellence.

BullsEYE Bullet: "There is no greater agony than bearing an untold story inside you."[23]

—Maya Angelou

HOW WRITING ELEVATES YOUR EXCELLENCE

To help shore up any reservations you may have about how reading a chapter about writing a daily journal or a book can contribute to elevating your excellence and leverage the power of doing ordinary things extraordinarily well, please consider the following benefits to connect the relevance for you:

Writing conditions you to stay in the moment
While you need to reflect upon the past for appropriate lessons to share and glance into the future for wise planning, the act of writing itself keeps you in the moment. When writing, you must focus on being where

your feet are and giving all you have to what you've got. In fact, writing can be so engaging that you become completely immersed in the task in front of you and lose all track of time. When writing, I've found from my own experience that what "flows is fab," and what's "forced is foul." But when it is flowing, and you're locked into the moment in front of your face, you are in a zone that you're in no hurry to leave and that you want to duplicate in other life arenas.

Writing helps you think logically and communicate effectively
Writing helps you organize your thoughts, think logically, and express yourself intelligently. Thus, writing well will improve your verbal communication skills as you upgrade your ability to communicate in a manner people understand, can follow, feel, and buy into. In this regard, writing makes you a more excellent communicator overall, not just through your written words.

Writing improves your attention to detail
When you write regularly, you pay more attention to detail and develop a greater appreciation for "how you do anything is how you do everything." You recognize the difference just a single word can mean in expressing a thought or adding value to an analogy. You become more aware of how to say more with less, using the details of punctuation properly to express your ideas well, and the importance of proper context and illustration to support and add color to what you communicate.

Writing helps you reflect and apply life lessons in the present moment
Rather than live in the past, you learn from it, evaluate it, embrace the lessons, and apply them to make the moment you're in more excellent and effective.

ELEVATE YOURSELF AND OTHERS: WRITE THE BOOK

Writing builds confidence
This is especially true if you've never enjoyed writing or haven't felt you were good at it, but you work through that initial hesitancy and discomfort and do it nonetheless. You feel better about yourself and your abilities when you take on and accomplish—if even in a small way or in modest steps—something you previously avoided, disliked, or dreaded. In this regard, writing becomes another win you can stack during your day, even if writing a few thoughts in your daily gratitude journal or diary.

Writing can lower stress levels
Negative thoughts or emotions often play on an unhealthy reel in our minds. This can make something already stressful even more so. But when you divert your attention from those things, many of which you can't control, and engage in a productive activity like writing that you can control, it can lessen the counterproductive thoughts by putting you back in control, gaining personal momentum, building morale, and returning to something productive. Writing allows you to get your thoughts out, rather than bottle them up within, which almost always mitigates the tension you're carrying around. I can't even count how many get-it-off-my-chest letters I've composed but never sent to others that allowed me to alleviate the pent-up frustration, anger, or tension I was carrying because of a relational conflict.

Writing creates a legacy that outlives you
When your time on Earth is finished, whatever you've written and leave behind you, whether published or not, will be part of a legacy that outlives you—one that shares your voice, lessons, ideas, views, joys, frustrations, observations, and experiences with future generations. In this

regard, writing can move you from being a successful person to a person of significance—one who continues to influence and impact beyond their years of physical presence. Even if your words only impact a single person, you will have elevated yourself beyond the ranks of so many who, when they die, it's as though they never lived, because the words of their unique experience never impacted other lives.

While these seven points don't offer a complete list of the benefits of writing or journaling regularly, they hopefully offer a compelling case for taking the task seriously. To supplement the aforementioned benefits, I'm including a few tips and thoughts to nudge you forward:

It doesn't matter if anyone else ever reads or even likes what you write
First and foremost, you're doing this for *you*, and the benefits of developing the discipline and improving your thoughts, confidence, attention to detail, and more are rewards enough to do it. In that regard, if anyone else reads and benefits from your words, it's nice but unnecessary.

You don't have to write much at once, just write something regularly
Like anything else, you get better with practice. So, it's not so much about how much you write, or even what you write, but that you write something, do the best possible job you can with it, and then make a habit of doing it consistently. Again, any type of daily journaling lends itself well to this and can build confidence and capacity to write blogs, manuals, e-books, and even novels.

It's not about getting published
If getting published is your goal, and it is a worthy one, then that is something you can certainly learn more about doing and work towards. But don't let the fact that "I'll never get it published" or "I wouldn't know

how to go through the process of writing a book or getting it to market" stop you from doing what you *can* do daily: writing your thoughts, experiences, lessons, plans, and more, in order to reap benefits like those I've listed.

Write your story

If you have a desire to write a history of your career thus far, or your life story, but don't know where to begin, it could be something as simple as starting with your life's ten biggest wins and lessons and your ten biggest regrets or mistakes: what you did, what you learned, who you became in the process, and more. Borrowing a baseball analogy: If a batter comes to the plate twenty times and gets ten hits, he's batting .500. You could make your own working title the same: "Batting 500." Write something every day. Update your wins and losses as they change over time. You're also likely to benefit from reflecting, remembering, and recommitting to behaviors or disciplines you once had but stopped, or by correcting missteps you're taking now as you recall what they cost you previously. If you'd like further insight and encouragement on this topic, listen to *The Game Changer Life* podcast episode 419, "Write the Book!"

◎ **BullsEYE Bullet:** "We write to taste life twice, in the moment and in retrospect."[24]

—Anaïs Nin

MY *PEAK:* JUST DO IT!

I've written books since 1998, and *Elevate Your Excellence* is my sixteenth work. Inevitably, when some people discuss their own book idea with me and lament over how they never made time to start, or list any number of other excuses for why they've never written the book they carry within them, some will ask a question such as, "With all you have to do, how have you found the time to write all those books?" My answer probably isn't what they're looking for, but once they consider it, they will likely understand the message I'm communicating. I reply, "The secret to writing the book is that you have to WRITE THE BOOK! Stop talking about it and start being about it!" There is no secret! Journals, blogs, books, and more don't write themselves.

Start with an outline, and don't overthink every aspect before you start. Much of the path evolves as you move forward. But you can't ever move forward if you don't start at all. There will never be a perfect time, and the thoughts in your head concerning what you'd like to write will unlikely ever be completely clear until you start putting them on paper. And therein lies the beauty of beginning. You can't take the second step until you take the first, but once that is done the path starts to become more defined.

If you have no interest in writing a book or don't have a compelling idea for what to write, then write your own story. No one knows it better than you. If that intimidates you, then start with a daily journal where you write a sentence, or paragraph or two, at day's end concerning your experiences, observations, feelings, and lessons, and that can perhaps become your story someday. If even that seems like too much of a demand on your time, then begin with filling in the five or six empty spaces in a daily gratitude journal during your morning mindset routine. What you write is less important than the fact that you do write something every day to reap the daily benefits that accompany writing.

BullsEYE Bullet: "Action is a great restorer and builder of confidence. Inaction is not only the result, but the cause, of fear."[25]

—**Norman Vincent Peale**

TAKE (5) RAPID REVIEW AND ACTION STEPS

1. Which of the listed benefits of writing regularly most appeal to you? If you already write consistently, which of the benefits, or other benefits not listed, has helped improve your thinking and elevate your excellence the most?
2. Do you have, or have you had in the past, ideas to write columns, stories, journals, a book, etc., that you've not started yet? What has stopped you? What's the one next right thing you can do to move from immobility to accomplishment?
3. If you've not formed a habit of writing regularly and see its value, where can you begin? When will you begin?
4. If you've written regularly in the past and got away from the habit, why was that? What did you learn that will help you to begin again and become more consistent going forward?
5. Considering the Norman Vincent Peale quote that concludes the chapter, is there a fear of writing that's held you back? A fear of failure, fear you won't stick with it, fear you won't enjoy or be good at it, or some other fear? Could working through that discomfort and overcoming the fear be the confidence boost you need to further elevate your own excellence? If yes, when will you begin?

Chapter Thirteen
ELEVATE EXCELLENCE IN YOUR INTERESTS

Have you ever been through a phase in your life when you didn't work to live, you lived to work? A time when you became so obsessed with your career that you tied your identity to how poorly or how well you did in that particular life arena, and where the focus on that career created casualties in other life arenas: family, friends, health, hobbies, spiritually, and more? A period when you weren't merely working but were being *worked;* not truly living but were just being *lived?* It happens. A lot. And maybe this is you right now. If that's the case, or if you don't want it to become your reality someday, then you may find this chapter liberating.

A lifelong commitment to elevating your excellence and doing ordinary things extraordinarily well can benefit you far beyond your career arena and add further value to your daily joy and enrichment by making life's everyday, routine tasks, events, or pastimes more meaningful and enjoyable. The fact is: Even the workaholic spends more time away from work than on the job most days, so maximizing those away-from-work moments and elevating excellence in your interests other than work can determine a significant aspect of your personal enrichment and fulfillment. That being said, a fair question is: Are you currently doing enough to elevate your excellence in your interests outside of work, and if not, what more could you do to leverage the power of doing ordinary things extraordinarily well? Otherwise, you may end up in a rut where, day after day, you are going through the motions in those life arenas, and thus, you are spending more of your waking hours committed to getting *through* things versus getting *from* them.

For instance, you likely eat meals or snacks several times per day, so perhaps learning more about eating intentionally, and about how food affects your body, mood, weight, longevity, and how it either contributes to illness or prevents it, would help you make better decisions about what you put into your body. You could become more strategic, more purposeful, and reap the benefits of that new discipline with each meal or snack during the day.

If you enjoy wine, take a course or read a book on wines: the various regions, grape varieties, how the terroir contributes to the taste, how to best pair wine with food, and more. Pick a particular region or country to immerse yourself in and develop a level of excellence—perhaps even expertise!

We all have preferred ways of taking in information. Personally, I'm partial to online courses, supplemented with supporting reading material for further study. My subscription to MasterClass, the online training portal where experts teach courses on a wide array of topics including food, the arts, business, leadership, and more, is an annual investment I highly value. I far prefer taking a couple of fifteen- to twenty-minute segments in an area of interest than watching another thirty-minute episode of a television program. The former helps me grow; the latter sometimes entertains me but mostly wastes my time. And since nothing is neutral in my life, choosing to grow rather than opting to be amused moves me closer to the person I'm trying to become and the life I aspire to live.

What you do to elevate your interests is up to you and will be determined naturally by your own passions, curiosities, and talents. In this chapter I'll share examples of courses I've taken and how I've benefited, not with the implication you should duplicate them, but with the hope it will encourage you to accelerate your own personal growth program in this regard, if you currently have one, or begin to explore elevating your excellence in areas where you regularly engage, if you do not. I've found it to be an incredibly effective way to make the most of each moment, associate with the activities that elevate me rather than devastate me—the activities that add value to me and make me more valuable in the process.

◎ **BullsEYE Bullet:** "Excellence is in the details. Give attention to the details in everything you do, and excellence will come."[26]

—**Perry Sexton**

AN *EYE* OPENER: FIRST HALF GROWTH OBJECTIVES

As part of my personal growth plan, I set quarterly growth objectives in areas related to my work, as well as in areas unrelated to vocation but where I have interest in developing knowledge and skill. I only share what is next to offer an actual example of what I've done recently, so readers can visualize how something similar may work for them, and not because I believe the steps I took are a prototype or model anyone else needs to follow. I'm including examples of the segment number and length of each program I took so you can see how this might have applied to you, and how you could have broken it down into manageable sessions in your downtime. Again, growth is a personal decision and should be customized around one's own strengths, needs, and interests. What I am presenting is simply about my own areas of interest I wished to elevate through intentional growth objectives. Make your own growth objectives about you!

My strategy: I prefer to budget blocks of time within a day to grow so I can get into a rhythm and dig deeper into the subject I'm studying. Once that time is scheduled, I can tune everything else out and give it the gift of my attention. While I used to read books only as part of my growth plan, and I still enjoy great reads, I've tweaked my disciplines to incorporate more of the new technology available 24/7 through online training courses. My past six months' worth of growth objectives included MasterClass.com courses on:

Leading Winning Teams by Coach Geno Auriemma
Fifteen lessons over two hours and fifty-two minutes

While teaching leadership and coaching principles is part of my own work with athletes and business professionals, I'm always looking for ways to improve and elevate my excellence in delivery, what I say, or how I can make it "make sense," and this course helped build on that strength.

The Art of Negotiation by Chris Voss
Eighteen lessons over three hours and four minutes

This course also relates to what I do for a living, but negotiating is a life skill that can apply in one way or another to every life arena. I'm very good at negotiation, and since it's easier to go from good to great in an area of skill or knowledge than from miserable to mediocre, Chris's methods gave me new insights into how to improve what I'm already good at and get better in several key negotiating tactics.

Strategic Decision-Making by Mellody Hobson
Ten lessons over one hour and thirty-eight minutes

This course helped me fine-tune a process I had already used to make personal and business decisions, and it added additional insights I can share to help clients facing tough calls. While related primarily to my work, it is also a life skill, just as the course on negotiation was. Courses that can elevate excellence across multiple life arenas are of particular interest to me.

Intentional Eating by Michael Pollan
Thirteen lessons over three hours and eighteen minutes

This area of my life has been a weakness—a topic I knew little about but wanted to expand my knowledge to not only improve my own life but to become more valuable to my family and clients and share what I've learned. It changed how I thought about food, what I ate, and as a result it improved my health, daily energy, and self-confidence.

Gardening by Ron Finley
Ten lessons over two hours and seven minutes

I've long enjoyed tinkering in the yard, and I get satisfaction out of partnering with our long-time gardener to improve our own property, which over the years has shaped into something akin to a botanical garden. Gardening seemed a natural extension of that passion, and after completing this course, my wife and I now have a project we enjoy together as we are currently growing twenty different herbs, fruits, and vegetables. This was a course we were also able to enjoy and learn from as we viewed segments together. And here's a small example of how elevating one's excellence in one area can impact excellence in others: I now include the mint and basil we grow in the garden into my already-excellent morning smoothie, making it even better.

Modern Italian Cooking by Massimo Bottura
Fourteen lessons over three hours and forty-six minutes

I love to cook, and while Italian dining is my preferred cuisine when eating out, I knew little of how to cook it with excellence until watching Massimo's videos. His passion and skill have also prompted me to visit his restaurant in Italy, as well as to rent his villa, which he makes available. My enhanced knowledge of Italian food also prompted me to find a better local Italian restaurant than I'd been enjoying and to elevate the quality and experience of my favorite meals out as well.

Wine Appreciation by James Suckling
Eleven lessons over two hours and twenty-two minutes

The only thing I really knew about wine before taking this course was that I preferred red over white. I had envied friends and associates who could read a restaurant wine list, order just the right bottle, explain its attributes, and pair it expertly with the food ordered. Thus, when I saw this course was available, I decided to give it a shot.

James Suckling has long been one of the world's top wine critics, and what I feared might be a snobby master class on wine appreciation turned out to be one of the most informative and enjoyable courses I've ever taken. Because of his insight and what I've learned, I'll never "routinely" drink a glass of wine again, but I will have an entirely new perspective concerning what went into making it, and what creates the experience it provides.

In addition to the aforementioned MasterClass courses, I also enjoyed two online courses from Hillsdale College, which broadened my knowledge to enhance my personal faith, feeding a passion I have for biblically based principles—a passion that led me to author two books on the subject: *How to Run Your Business by THE BOOK* and *How to Lead by THE BOOK*.

The Life of King David by Professor Justin A. Jackson
Eight segments over three hours and forty-six minutes.

Exceptional insights regarding this unique biblical figure and icon of Jewish history.

Ancient Christianity by Dr. Kenneth Calvert
Eleven segments over five hours and twenty-six minutes

This course was evidence that you think you know a lot until you learn how much you still don't know. I'll watch it again to make sure I maximize Professor Calvert's expertise.

During this six-month period, I also read several exceptional faith-based books by my friend Gary Keesee. I highly recommend his entire The Kingdom series.

As you can see from my growth objective selections, some of my areas of interest I aspired to elevate were related primarily to my profession, while others fed an array of various passions or interests, and others still overlapped and would elevate my excellence in multiple life arenas. Again, this is what worked well for me. I include it as an example, not as a blueprint. You've got to do you!

From my own perspective, the time I spent viewing, reading, taking notes, and further researching the lessons learned brought greater value to my life than mindless web or channel surfing, video games, fantasy football, bingeing on Netflix or the Food Network, and the like. Your preferences may differ, but the undergirding principle for me remained the same throughout my choices for how to use my time: Since nothing I engaged in would have a neutral impact on my life, I picked activities I felt would best simultaneously move me towards my goals, stack wins, and elevate my excellence. And incidentally, if you enjoy and benefit from online courses, you can find over two hundred hours' worth amongst dozens of categories either instantly downloadable at the Dave on Demand section of www.learntolead.com or by subscribing to one of the many packages available in our Online Training category at that same website. Essentially, my entire life's work of video training is available on that portal.

◎ **BullsEYE Bullet:** "Do you know great minds enjoy excellence, average minds love mediocrity and small minds adore comfort zones?"[27]

—Onyi Anyado

CHECKLIST FOR ELEVATING YOUR INTERESTS

Following are suggestions to help you elevate your interests, your excellence, and to reap more of the power that comes with doing ordinary things extraordinarily well:

Know how you learn best
The best way to learn is however you learn best. It may be visually through reading or viewing, or you may have better auditory intelligence and listening to messages resonates with you best. Your optimal method may be kinesthetic, where you learn optimally by interacting and doing

what you're learning in a hands-on forum. It may be a combination of all of these.

Set specific growth objectives
Set specific, time-based objectives that appeal to your strengths, passions, interests, or that improve weakness. This kind of clarity provides a benchmark for focus, pace, and allows you to measure progress and hold yourself accountable. Set the time-based growth objectives that work best for you. I prefer monthly or quarterly because they are shorter in duration and put more "pressure" on doing something now, whereas longer-term goals can remove the incentive for short-term urgency or consistency.

Decide how to best resource your growth objectives
As I've mentioned, I enjoy online courses, supported by books for further research. You may do likewise, or instead prefer to attend live classes, or listen to audio books or podcasts. There is normally no shortage of resources to support a growth goal, so choose whatever helps you best. I would also suggest you cut your losses if you've chosen a course or book that just doesn't click with you. Time is too precious to wade through poor choices in the name of "consistency." Move on to something that makes more sense and moves you forward.

Budget time to improve
You're more likely to follow your growth plan if you schedule or set aside time to improve, rather than trying to squeeze the time into your schedule if an opening magically appears. Be more intentional than incidental in this regard, and you'll increase the likelihood that your plan is executed consistently. If you get off track in your growth disciplines, and most likely you will at some point, get back on track as quickly as possible. Don't allow dips to become ditches.

Apply and/or share what you learn as soon as possible

The sooner you can apply what you learn, the faster you'll own it and move on to mastery. As soon as I completed Coach Auriemma's online course on leading teams, I incorporated lessons into a podcast and shared his principles in a live seminar. Halfway through James Suckling's wine appreciation course, I bought specific bottles and did tastings to experience what he was teaching. We bought gardening materials and planted our first "crop" within days after completing Ron's course on gardening, and I taught my revised decision-making process to a struggling athlete within a week after refining it, and he was able to make a decision he'd been stuck on for two months in just twenty-four hours. Remember that the objective of growth isn't to become a warehouse of never-used knowledge but to build your capacity to relentlessly execute in the life arenas most relevant to you fulfilling your aspirations.

Keep growing and going

Enjoy your growth journey! The completion of a book or course is in one sense an ending but is also a beginning to a new opportunity to learn, acquire, or improve skills; elevate your interests and your excellence; become more valuable; and add more value. It's unlikely you could say the same about investing those same hours working on yourself as you could about putting like time into playing Candy Crush or online poker, or consuming hours of reality television.

MY *PEAK:* FROM EXCELLENCE TO EXPERTISE

While I have a variety of growth objectives where I'd like to elevate my excellence, I understand that I am limited by time as to how many of them I can dig into as deeply as I'd like and develop expertise. You will likely find the same in your personal development pursuits. From the good and the great options where you want to elevate your excellence, you must choose the *best* option if you aspire to develop genuine expertise. And there is a big difference between excellence and expertise. You may be excellent in a variety of areas but will likely have expertise in a very select few—perhaps just one. Let me explain further: After my dad's mom remarried, he was adopted by a William Anderson, a good and kind man who raised him as his own. My father's birth dad, however, was Fredo Cipriani, who arrived in the United States from Sicily in the 1920s. While I look more like my Irish mom, my dad and one of my brothers have physical attributes resembling native Sicilians. This heritage may explain my love of Italian food, clothing, and my interest in improving my expertise in the twenty Italian wine regions and their corresponding grapes, terroirs, and wines. Yes, I also enjoy bourbon and ryes, but the history of wine fascinates me, especially Italian wine, and resonates well with my family heritage. To fuel my "expertise" growth objective, I am taking an intensive Italian Wine Scholar course, have joined the Italian wine guild, and have other steps planned for the future.

You may have no particular desire to elevate your excellence to expertise in either a vocational area or one that is related to another life arena. However, if there is a passion nudging you in that regard, I can suggest three things based on my own experience:

- Pursuing or upgrading expertise will change and enrich your life in many facets.
- Keep your focus narrow. You can do *anything* but not *everything*.
- Your journey is never complete, so buckle in for the long haul, stay hungry and humble, and enjoy the ride.

◎ **BullsEYE Bullet:** "Never become so much of an expert that you stop gaining expertise. View life as a continuous learning experience."[28]

—Denis Waitley

TAKE (5) RAPID REVIEW AND ACTION STEPS

1. Do you currently have time-based growth objectives for knowledge, a skill, an attitude upgrade, a habit, or more?
2. Do you have growth objectives in both vocational areas and other life arenas?
3. If you have growth objectives to elevate your excellence, do you budget time to improve, and have you properly resourced those objectives? Are you just interested in them, or committed to them?
4. If you don't have effective growth objectives, what could yours be?
5. Is there currently an area of your life you'd like to elevate from "excellence to expertise?" What is it?

Chapter Fourteen

MAKE *EDMED* A LIFESTYLE

I used to buy good books I never finished, start better habits that fizzled in time, and begin new diets and soon see them derailed by my need for instant gratification. In the workplace, I'd launch new processes, initiatives, or practices that would work as long as I worked them, but I would nonetheless stop working them! I struggled with consistency for years. I was a good "starter," quick to make decisions and decide to go for something, but sticking with it over the course of time, especially when results didn't come fast enough, was a persistent challenge. Even when I got results in reasonable time, the ensuing arrogance of success would affect my resolve to continue them. I thought "I've just never been a consistent person," when a better analysis would have been: "I need to learn the skill of becoming more consistent, but primarily I must have stronger reasons for why being inconsistent is no longer an option."

Suffice it to say there were hundreds of these fizzle-out failures over several decades on the journey to understanding and embracing the EDMED (Every Day Means Every Day) mindset and eventually converting **EDMED** into a lifestyle. As this book comes close to concluding, consider that starting new disciplines or implementing fresh ideas you've learned throughout these chapters is the easy part. The real work begins in the trenches of day-to-day execution, when you're pounded by conditions you can't control and prone to surrender to emergencies of the moment. It's during those times especially that you need an EDMED mindset that can grow into an EDMED lifestyle, powering you to consistently build and sustain greater excellence in all your life arenas.

AN *EYE* OPENER: THE HIJACKED GARDEN

Our newly planted garden provided a poignant lesson of how quickly what is in excellent shape can degrade seemingly overnight when you stop consistently paying attention to the details that create excellence. My wife, Rhonda, and I had recently planted twenty different herbs, fruits, and vegetables while I was in town for a thirty-day stretch—allowing me to tend to it daily after returning home from our office each afternoon. I find working outdoors relaxing, and I looked forward to my daily garden rendezvous and was encouraged to see how well it progressed after the first few weeks of planting.

The day before embarking on a two-day, five-city speaking tour, I inspected our work and was delighted that everything appeared in optimal shape. It was beautiful! I told Rhonda that since our gardener was scheduled to come the following day he'd take care of the garden, leaving only the day after for her to pull garden duty. She had *one* job I requested of her. For *one* day. And she forgot. To exacerbate matters, our gardener forgot as well, and upon my return I discovered our one-time Garden of Eden had less life than the Dead Sea. Tomato branches sagged like my aging eyelids, the cucumber leaves were riddled with dime-sized holes, okra plants were dead on my arrival, and grotesque slugs feasted on the basil I put in my morning smoothie. This decline took roughly sixty hours to manifest. To further my aggravation, after discussing with Rhonda her failure to execute that *one* job and suggesting I should perhaps terminate her partnership in our garden project and its forthcoming fruits, she casually reminded me, regardless of what happened, that by law she'd still own 50 percent of the garden and fully intended to haul off the best half of each harvest.

Many of your own routines and essential disciplines are like that garden: If they're not tended to daily, they naturally wind down; they don't take care of themselves or improve on their own. If you struggle staying consistent with the changes you initiate or the projects you begin, then making EDMED a lifestyle can be your greatest ally. If you excel at the critical success factor of consistency in excellence, EDMED will sustain you.

> **BullsEYE Bullet:** Anything of excellence is built daily, not in a day. And *every* day means *every* day.

THE *EDMED* ACRONYM

One of the most consistently high-performing leaders I've worked with over the years is the automotive industry's Flavio Galasso from Naples, Florida. With our mutual backgrounds in martial arts, we connected easily, and I recognized early on that his no-nonsense approach to daily execution and accountability was a key factor setting him apart. For years I heard him repeat the mantra "every day means every day" when speaking to his team on the importance of executing key disciplines and duties. He lived that principle personally, which gave him increased credibility to expect it from others. I liked the simplicity of "every day means every day" so well that I took Flavio's signature phrase and created an acronym: EDMED.

EDMED embodies the unflinching consistency that builds excellence and greatness in our lives. It also helps prevent regression in our performance like one mitigates decline in a garden by attending to a few key disciplines daily. What I like most about EDMED is its emphasis on *daily*, not occasionally, executing the most effective decisions and disciplines to move you towards your personal and professional goals. EDMED starts as a mindset and, over time, it can become part of your nature—a lifestyle. It is about moving from a passing interest to a firm commitment to reach the goals mattering most to you. EDMED requires incredible self-control because, frankly, if you're like I am, there are many days you don't *feel* like doing the right things: eating healthy, getting up early to work out, initiating the required phone calls, sinking hundreds of three-point shots on the court after you've practiced two hours, studying for the test, making your bed, or any of the other dozens of tasks, routines, or rituals discussed in this book or that are relevant to your own life. For many people, EDMED is demoted to an occasional or situational thing: they become consistent in right decisions and disciplines when they have to or if they feel up to it, when time is running out, and often when things are falling apart and they need to get back on track.

This chapter discusses how to develop the EDMED lifestyle in all your vital life arenas. In fact, you may discover that you are one of the multitudes who are just one consistent discipline away from an entirely different level healthwise, financially, in your workplace, sport, within a relationship, or more.

> ◎ **BullsEYE Bullet:** When your dreams are bigger than your excuses, EDMED can become a lifestyle, as you view consistency as a privilege not punishment.

THE "SEPARATOR" FROM *UNSTOPPABLE*

In my book *Unstoppable*, I present four types of mindsets related to, and reflected in, one's performance: undertaker, caretaker, playmaker, and game changer. While I won't go into extensive details concerning the nuances of each group here, I do want to focus on the two best performance groups: the playmaker and game changer.

As I outlined in that book, these two types of performers have a lot in common as it relates to making right decisions and executing effective disciplines, but what separates them most often is that the game changer does those right things more consistently. They've made EDMED more of a lifestyle. They have learned to subordinate their feelings in the moment to creating a better moment in their future. They have developed consistency, and the *developing* aspect is hopeful news for anyone aspiring to become more consistent because that inconsistency isn't a fixed state but can be elevated into consistency with intentional effort and conditioning. After all, "consistency" isn't a gene you're born with, nor is it something you learn in a book or that can be effectively developed over the long term by external cajoling, bribing, begging, or threatening. Rather, it is a force that comes from within, starting with your thinking and manifesting in behaviors. You may recall we covered this to a degree in chapter six, and to save you the time finding that particular passage on consistency, I've repeated it here for reinforcement:

Consistency is key

You wouldn't expect to build an elite body by doing five push-ups on the days you felt like it, then declaring yourself "fit for life." Nor can we build an elite mindset following the same "do it when it's convenient" or "if I feel like it" precursors to inconsistency. Many people bail out prematurely on a new discipline or activity because they're not getting a fast-enough positive consequence or payoff. They don't stick with the process long enough for the compounding effect of right decisions and disciplines done with excellence to change their lives. In many cases, they don't have strong enough reasons to stick with the discipline, so they give themselves the option of quitting. This is where that compelling *why* positively influences your consistency. When there is a certain type of person you're trying to become, a goal or dream you crave achieving, or a difference you long to make that burns intensely, consistency will be easier, because your aspirations are so powerful you can't afford to be inconsistent. You won't give yourself the option not to do what you need to do, because you so strongly desire what you want that you must do it.

Considering these thoughts, you may safely say that the root difference influencing the disparity in behavior between the playmaker and game changer isn't the strength of their will but the power of their *why;* their personal reasons for doing what's right and effective, for living EDMED, even on the days it's inconvenient, costly, or hard—because their reasons for doing it are so compelling they've not allowed themselves the luxury to opt out of it. Another way of looking at this is: despite protestations to the contrary concerning how badly someone professes to want something, if they are inconsistent in the decisions and disciplines needed to achieve that something, they simply don't want it badly enough.

> **◎ BullsEYE Bullet:** "Consistency is what transforms average into excellence. Small daily improvements are the key to staggering long-term results!"[29]
> —Syed Balkhi

EIGHT HELPS TO CONSISTENCY

Following are eight insights and actions you can take to improve your consistency.

Manage your expectations from the outset
There is no prize in life without a price, and the price you pay for growth in consistency, excellence, and results isn't a lump sum but an installment plan with no "final payment due." Understand that developing consistency and making EDMED a lifestyle is a process that forms over time and not overnight. By beginning any new process, routine, ritual, or more with realistic expectations and with a long-haul mindset uncompromised by the need for instant gratification, you're more likely to weather the storms of disappointments, delays, or setbacks throughout your journey and persist.

Create a *why* worth fighting for
You're unlikely to persevere or fight hard enough or long enough for goals you're indifferent about or are okay if you miss! This is why it's important to review your *why* often, preferably daily as part of your

mindset routine, so you don't lose sight of why you're doing what you're doing. You float adrift when your goals get covered in fog. This is why it's also important to keep your reasons relevant and compelling. As life changes, so too may your priorities and aspirations. You simply won't put in the work necessary to achieve something that matters somewhat, or that used to matter a lot, versus something that matters the most now.

Evaluate and adjust quickly
You may recall in chapter four that I discussed the importance of holding yourself accountable daily. This is a theme I can't stress enough. To review and reinforce what that entails, I'm including the passage here I'm referring to for a quick review:

Hold yourself accountable daily for your success in executing your Max Acts
This is a good place to share some insight into this discipline. Holding yourself accountable should go beyond whether or not you executed your priorities and should also consider how well you stayed flexible and adjusted when conditions beyond your control changed. But first and foremost, in order to hold yourself accountable, you'll need to start with clarity because clarity enables accountability; otherwise, the question becomes "Accountable for what?" This is why by beginning the day with your priorities pre-established and narrowed down, you create for yourself a benchmark for "game filming" your performance at day's end. This is simply spending a few minutes reflecting and noticing where you did well, so you can reinforce and duplicate the behaviors that enabled those wins, as well as recognizing

where you fell short so you can evaluate, adjust, and be more effective tomorrow. Incidentally, this brief daily game film is an effective use of visiting the past for appropriate lessons in order to make your coming present moments more effective.

You may also enjoy and benefit from a *The Game Changer Life* podcast episode I did on this topic. It is episode number 387 and aptly titled "How to Hold Yourself More Accountable."

Don't blame
Blame is the language of victims and losers, so when you get off track in any vital process or routine, look for solutions not scapegoats. In other words, take responsibility, find a mirror, and fix what you can control. Focus on what you could have decided more intelligently and executed better, and do that moving forward.

Start a stop-doing list
Decide which actions or associations you'll need to spend less time with or renounce altogether to buy back the time you'll need to do what's most essential. Don't let the "fun," trivial, and amusing hijack the essential—and your life's potential—because what's truly fun is changing your life, helping others change theirs, leaving a legacy, and winning bigger and more often.

Get better at what you do
An underrated secret to consistency is confidence. Frankly, if you feel better about yourself and your abilities when you do something, and you see better results because of that confidence, you're more likely to do those things consistently. People tend to avoid doing what they don't feel

comfortable or confident doing, or when they suffer frustration, rejection, or failure. In this regard, confidence is a conduit to consistency.

Know how to fall in love
The key is to fall in love with the goals you have and not to worry about whether or not you love or even like what it takes to get there: the tasks, routines, rituals, sacrifices, or processes. You don't have to fall in love with those things, just fall in love with where they'll take you and what they can do for you, and those things will become more lovable! What you'll often find is that as you begin to get results that change your life, you're now actually enjoying the price you once felt you were paying—if even in an odd sort of love-hate way.

Understand the difference between hunger and commitment
Action is evidence of commitment. A lot of people will say how much they "want it," or talk about how hungry they are, but they don't take the consistent, excellent action to get what they profess to crave.

It's like a guy who really wants to ask a certain girl out on a date or who's hungry for a promotion at work. He has an intense desire to be with her, or he thinks he deserves that promotion, but in either case he won't leave his comfort zone and take the action step to make it happen. He's certainly interested in the girl or promotion, but he's not committed enough to do what it takes to convert his aspiration into reality.

Don't get me wrong. Hunger is important, and it can get you started, but commitment is what helps you fight through the discomfort and finish. The world abounds with hungry and driven people who die broke, unfulfilled, or embarrassed because they were never committed enough to act and change their state, take a risk, make themselves uncomfortable, forego instant gratification, or bounce back when they took a step back. Excellent, uncomfortable, EDMED action validates your hunger far more than words or mantras. There comes a time when you've got to stop *talking* about it and start *being* about it.

> 🎯 **BullsEYE Bullet:** Lock like a laser on your goals but know that you won't enjoy all that's involved in getting there. Nor would you enjoy getting stuck in a comfort zone and missing your best life either.

MY *PEAK:* WEIGH YOURSELF DAILY

For years, despite having a goal weight of 200 pounds, my weight fluctuated between 220 and 240 pounds. Because of my height, my additional girth wasn't terribly obvious to most people, but I could certainly tell the difference, especially in how my seminar suits would fit. I tried a variety of diets and would lose the necessary pounds—sticking with the process until I reached my goal weight—but would then slowly get away from the disciplines that created a better outcome and find myself back squeezing into my suit and hoping the audience didn't call me out publicly when I spoke to them about topics like discipline and commitment.

A doctor had suggested I hold myself accountable by weighing on the same day each week, and he explained how weighing more often could "mess with my mind" because of wide daily fluctuations caused by bloating, water weight, travel, and more. The problem with the weekly "Monday morning weigh-in" was that it took the pressure off me sticking to my disciplines as rigidly between Monday evening through Thursday. Far too often we'd be out at dinner on Monday evening, and when the server brought the dessert cart by our table, it was easy for me to rationalize "I don't have to weigh again for another entire week. If I 'reward' myself tonight with that chocolate cheesecake and strawberry topping, I'll have plenty of time to make up for it and take the weight back off in time for next Monday's weigh-in." And then on Taco Tuesday, when I had downed three and was considering a fourth taco, I'd rationalize, "Well, I still have five days before I weigh, and one more taco isn't that big of a deal," which may have been true had I not already eaten three! And the fact was I wouldn't make up for the ground I'd given up, but at best I would ensure I didn't lose further ground by sticking with the diet the remaining days. Waiting too long in between the Monday accountability sessions on the scale didn't work for me. And while I fully understood the doctor recommending a weekly weigh-in because of the back-and-forth way the body carries and loses weight from day to day, I also understood a more powerful factor: the power that shorter-term goals and more rapid accountability has on your psyche, sense of urgency, and decision-making. And so I started weighing daily, every single day, and EDMED. I took into account there could be wide daily fluctuations for bloating, water weight, and more based on my lifestyle during that day. However, I more greatly appreciated the incentive I'd have to make right decisions and stick with productive disciplines at every meal, and in between meals, if I knew I'd be hauling myself onto a scale within a matter of hours, weighing each morning, and facing the consequences or enjoying the rewards of my past behaviors faster. To improve daily accountability further, I also recorded each day's weight in the appropriate daily space in my gratitude journal. The EDMED philosophy for weighing myself worked for me, and my daily appointment with accountability on my scale each day managed my decisions and disciplines for me. I lost thirty-eight pounds and have now fluctuated between 195 and 200 pounds—a goal I thought completely unreasonable years ago—for several years running. I don't have a fixed diet, nor do I count calories. I'm just incentivized to make better decisions because I weigh myself each day. The EDMED mindset created a lifestyle change that went beyond quick fixes or fads, and it will for you too in any area you want to improve—or where you need to upgrade your behaviors from occasionally to consistently.

Please don't miss that the point of this section isn't for me to try and teach anyone how to lose weight. And although this discipline may help you as it did me, I have zero expertise in weight loss. But accountability is an expertise, and what I do want to illustrate is the power that shorter-term accountability can have to positively influence your EDMED mindset and lead you to make better decisions in every moment. And "weighing yourself daily" goes far beyond managing the daily decisions and disciplines to influence your physical weight, and it can apply to any daily priorities you set that you want to hold yourself immediately accountable for to reinforce where you're on track and correct your course more quickly when you deviate. Starting the day with scheduled priorities and evaluating at day's end where you fell short or were successful is a simple and effective form of weighing yourself daily. Going into a meeting with specific objectives and evaluating your success or failure in each aspect afterwards is another example. Find your own ways and life arenas to weigh yourself daily, and you'll take a leap forward in developing the EDMED mindset you need to elevate your excellence and do the ordinary things extraordinarily well.

◎ **BullsEYE Bullet:** "Success isn't a destination thing, it's a daily thing."[30]

—**John C. Maxwell**

MAKE A NEW END

After three decades of speaking professionally, it's common for an attendee to tell me some version of this after a presentation: "I wish

I'd have heard you twenty years ago." Maybe. Maybe not. Many of the things I teach today I didn't know twenty years ago! There's a chance as this book nears its end you may think something similar concerning some of the strategies you've learned. But as the saying goes, "While you can't go back and start over again, you can start now and make a new end." Because of this, both your opportunity and your challenge become answering questions like these:

With fourteen chapters of strategies to consider, where do I start?
How many of these ideas can I implement at once?
Which are essential that I should start now if I haven't already?
Which are important, but not essential, that I can weave into my life after the essential priorities have taken root?
How can I stick with the action I initiate this time?

Below is a summary of the chapter titles you've completed. Perhaps you've already begun to implement some of them, and others are still on your mental drawing board. Scan the notes from each chapter and list here, or in a notebook, the key point(s) you will implement to elevate your excellence. From some chapters you may have several key points, and with others nothing may have resonated that makes you want to change what you're doing currently.

Then prioritize them. Perhaps separate them into three or four strategic waves with two to three manageable items in each wave, and then begin to implement them at an acceptable rate of velocity that balances out doing enough to overwhelm the status quo holding you back without becoming overwhelmed, spreading yourself too thin, and watching your good intentions fizzle into the daily fray. There isn't a right or wrong place to start; there's just a right place for you. Everyone has different situations, strengths, opportunities, and weaknesses they must factor into any prioritized plan of action. Situation dictates strategy. Considering your own situation, you can begin to strategize accordingly in the space below. I wish you massive joy, success, impact, and fulfillment on your journey!

Chapter Title Summaries: Key Action Takeaways

1. The "Little" Things Aren't Little Things

2. Nothing Is Neutral

3. Start Early Stacking Wins

4. Master the Moment in Front of Your Face

5. Resuscitate Daily Routines and Rituals

6. Take Ten for Mindset Mastery

7. How to Have Good "Crappy" Days

8. Drink Up!

9. Intentional Breathing Adds Life to Your Years

10. Masterful Sleeping Adds Years to Your Life

11. Challenge Yourself

12. Elevate Yourself and Others: Write the Book

13. Elevate Excellence in Your Interests

14. Make EDMED a Lifestyle

◎ **BullsEYE Bullet:** "If you can change your mind, you can change your life."[31]

—**William James**

TAKE ⑤ RAPID REVIEW AND ACTION STEPS

1. In which of your important life arenas have you gotten off track in your daily disciplines? What's the next one right thing now that you can do to correct your course?
2. Is there an aspect of your *why* that needs strengthening or clarifying so that being inconsistent is no longer an option? Is your *why* relevant enough? Do you review it often enough?
3. Are there factors beyond your control that you routinely blame for your inconsistency, and can you see how that isn't working for you? Which aspect of those shortfalls can you begin to take responsibility for?
4. Do you begin each day with clear enough daily priorities so that you are able to hold yourself accountable as you "game film" at day's end? Do you schedule your priorities and work your day around them, or do you tend to try and squeeze your priorities into your day as it goes along? If so, how is that working for you? How can you do better?
5. Which aspects of your life would lend themselves to, and benefit from, your own version of "weighing yourself daily"? Is it possible you hold yourself more accountable for desired outcomes than you do for the daily decisions and disciplines most predictive of creating those outcomes? If yes, how can you tighten that up and become more accountable for living the EDMED lifestyle most predictive of creating those desired outcomes?

ACKNOWLEDGMENTS

Special thanks and recognition go out to the following team members who pulled together to make this work possible:

Matt Holt and his incredibly competent and engaged publishing team.

Sam Griesel, for sharing his tragic story that became a triumph.

Ryan "The Killer" Cota, for his indispensable expertise in editing, copy editing, and all-around in-house champion role behind this project.

Hannah Peacock, for doing the work of three running LearnToLead while Ryan and I were otherwise engaged with *Elevate Your Excellence*.

NOTES

1. "Denis Waitley Quotes," BrainyQuote. Accessed July 26, 2023. https://www.brainyquote.com/quotes/denis_waitley_146933.
2. John Wooden, Goodreads. Accessed June 28, 2023. https://www.goodreads.com/quotes/7018006-perfection-is-what-you-are-striving-for-but-perfection-is.
3. Damian Lillard (@Dame_Lillard), Twitter (X) post, January 14, 2015, 5:04 PM. https://twitter.com/Dame_Lillard/status/555485512492785665?lang=en.
4. Jim Rohn, AZQuotes.com. Accessed August 10, 2023. https://www.azquotes.com/quote/521047.
5. "Vince Lombardi Quotes," BrainyQuote. Accessed June 28, 2023. https://www.brainyquote.com/quotes/vince_lombardi_385070.
6. John C. Maxwell, Goodreads. Accessed March 21, 2024. https://www.goodreads.com/quotes/2312803-you-ll-never-change-your-life-until-you-change-something-you.
7. Jim Rohn Official (@OfficialJimRohn), Twitter (X) post, December 19, 2017, 2:30 PM. https://twitter.com/OfficialJimRohn/status/943201946382602241?ref_src=twsrc%5Egoogle%7Ctwcamp%5Eserp%7Ctwgr%5Etweet.
8. Tom Ziglar, *Choose to Win* (Nashville: Thomas Nelson Publishing, 2019), 191.

NOTES

9. Tiffany A. Ito et al., "Negative Information Weighs More Heavily on the Brain: The Negativity Bias in Evaluative Categorizations," *Journal of Personality and Social Psychology* 75, no. 4 (January 1, 1998): 887–900.
10. "Theodore Roosevelt Quotes," BrainyQuote. Accessed August 10, 2020, www.brainyquote.com/quotes/theodore_roosevelt_120663.
11. Sam Griesel, e-mail message to author, July 14, 2023.
12. Michael Hyatt, Goodreads. Accessed July 28, 2023. www.goodreads.com/quotes/10384144-you-lose-your-way-when-you-lose-your-why#:~:text=Quote%20by%20Michael%20Hyatt%3A%20%E2%80%9CYou,when%20you%20lose%20your%20why%E2%80%9D.
13. "Bobby Knight Quotes," BrainyQuote. Accessed August 2, 2023. https://www.brainyquote.com/quotes/bobby_knight_378526.
14. Kory Taylor, "Adult Dehydration," StatPearls—NCBI Bookshelf, October 3, 2022, https://www.ncbi.nlm.nih.gov/books/NBK555956/.
15. Ana Adán, "Cognitive Performance and Dehydration," *Journal of the American College of Nutrition* 31, no. 2 (April 1, 2012): 71–78, https://doi.org/10.1080/07315724.2012.10720011.
16. M. H. Cottle, "The work, ways, positions and patterns of nasal breathing (relevance in heart and lung illness," in *Rhinology: The collected writings of Maurice H. Cottle*, MD, ed. P. Barelli, W.E.E. Loch, E.R. Kern, and A. Steiner (American Rhinologic Society, 1987).
17. J.O.N. Lundberg and E. Weitzberg, "Nasal nitric oxide in man." *Thorax* 54, no. 10 (1999): 947–952.
18. American Lung Association, "Lung Capacity and Aging." Accessed October 30, 2023. https://www.lung.org/lung-health-diseases/how-lungs-work/lung-capacity-and-aging.
19. Henry David Thoreau, AZQuotes.com. Accessed August 3, 2023. https://www.azquotes.com/quote/294052.
20. NFL on ESPN (@ESPNNFL), Twitter (X) post, September 13, 2014, 9:00 AM. https://twitter.com/ESPNNFL/status/510774933278846976?lang=en.
21. Henry Ford, AZQuotes.com. Accessed August 3, 2023. https://www.azquotes.com/quote/397189.

NOTES

22. Zig Ziglar, AZQuotes.com. Accessed August 3, 2023. https://www.azquotes.com/quote/1426079.
23. Maya Angelou, AZQuotes.com. Accessed August 3, 2023. https://www.azquotes.com/quote/8497.
24. Anaïs Nin, AZQuotes.com. Accessed August 3, 2023. https://www.azquotes.com/quote/344221.
25. Norman Vincent Peale, AZQuotes.com. Accessed August 3, 2023. https://www.azquotes.com/quote/227553.
26. Perry Sexton, Goodreads. Accessed August 3, 2023. https://www.goodreads.com/author/quotes/8225761.
27. Onyi Anyado, Goodreads. Accessed August 3, 2023. https://www.goodreads.com/quotes/4463458-do-you-know-great-minds-enjoy-excellence-average-minds-love.
28. "Denis Waitley Quotes," BrainyQuote. Accessed July 26, 2023. https://www.brainyquote.com/quotes/denis_waitley_146933.
29. Syed Balkhi (@syedbalkhi), Twitter (X), March 1, 2022. https://twitter.com/syedbalkhi/status/1498652989317332994?lang=en.
30. John C. Maxwell, AZQuotes.com. Accessed August 3, 2023. https://www.azquotes.com/quote/656661.
31. William James, AZQuotes.com. Accessed August 3, 2023. https://www.azquotes.com/quote/365738.

ABOUT THE AUTHOR

Photo by Hannah Peacock

Dave Anderson, "Mr. Accountability," is a leading international speaker and author on elevating personal and team excellence. Since founding LearnToLead with his wife, Rhonda, in 1999, Dave has authored sixteen books and speaks more than one hundred times annually. Thousands have benefited from attending his live events, including individuals and teams from a wide array of businesses, athletics, and nonprofits. His hit podcast, *The Game Changer Life*, is heard by listeners in over 174 countries, and he has a diverse audience worldwide that engages him for team and one-on-one virtual coaching sessions over Zoom (everyone from business professionals to collegiate and professional athletes, and more), where together with Dave they can dive deeper into principles and strategies to help them grow themselves and others around them.

Dave and Rhonda reside in Southern California, where Dave conducts public workshops year-round at the LearnToLead corporate offices and intimate Elite Center training venue located in Agoura Hills, also home to their Matthew 25:35 Foundation.

WHAT'S NEXT?

Do you want to keep growing and going forward on your journey to elevate your excellence?

Visit www.learntolead.com for:

- Free videos and articles at our Insider's Club
- Our upcoming seminar schedule
- Virtual coaching opportunities with Dave on Zoom
- Hundreds of educational and motivational video downloads
- Information on how to bring Dave live to speak to your group: events@learntolead.com or call 818-735-9503

Following us on social media at:

- X (formerly Twitter): @learntolead100
- Instagram: @learntolead100
- LinkedIn: www.linkedin.com/in/daveandersonlearntolead/
- Facebook: @thegamechangerlife